AYURVEDA WISDOM

AYURVEDA

WISDOM

Cybèle Tomlinson

CONARI PRESS
Berkeley, California

Conari Press books are distributed by Publishers Group West.

Cover Photograph © Nancy Brown/ImageBank
Cover design: Suzanne Albertson
Book design: Claudia Smelser

ISBN: 1-57324-716-2

Library of Congress Cataloging-in-Publication Data

Tomlinson, Cybèle.
Ayurveda wisdom / Cybèle Tomlinson
p   cm.—(Simple wisdom book)
Includes bibliographical references and index.
ISBN 1-57324-716-2
1. Medicine, Ayurvedic. I. Title. II. Series.
R605 .T66 2002
615.5'3—dc21   2001005873
Printed in the United States of America on recycled paper.
02 03 04 05 Haddon   10 9 8 7 6 5 4 3 2 1

In memory of my father,

Michael Bangs Tomlinson

AYURVEDA WISDOM

PREFACE

I discovered Ayurveda many years ago when I was wandering in a tiny bookstore in Gloucester, Massachusetts, and stumbled on an intriguing Indian cookbook that used Ayurvedic principles. Since it was a cookbook, its focus was, of course, food. But what was different about it, and what was especially appealing to me, was the idea that food could be used for healing the body and bringing the mind into a more balanced state. This was exactly what I was already trying to do through my yoga practice. Later, as I explored a little further, I discovered that yoga and Ayurveda were actually two different branches of the same tradition.

After that early introduction to healthful cooking, it became clear to me that Ayurveda involved a great deal more than food. Ayurveda is a whole philosophy of life that encompasses just about every aspect of day-to-day living, including how we sleep, work, exercise, think, communicate, and many other things. It is meant to help us achieve the highest possible state of health, and its methods are simple, practical, and natural. I have found that the more I explore this vast system of healing, the more I am able to integrate it into my life in ways that are extremely helpful.

For instance, if I feel that I'm getting a cold, I can take certain herbs that will help me ward it off, or I can choose particular foods that will help bolster my immune system. If I find myself becoming overly energized, Ayurveda helps me understand why and provides me with an array of techniques for calming myself so that I feel more balanced. At the present time, I am pregnant, and during my pregnancy, I've been able to make dietary adjustments, take herbs, and practice more self-massage, one of the self-care techniques recommended in an Ayurvedic lifestyle. Best of all, Ayurveda deepens my understanding of myself and helps me structure regular, healthful routines into my life in such a way that I am likely to stay strong, fit, and balanced most of the time.

Many people associate Ayurveda with the beauty products and spa treatments that have recently become available, and these do, indeed, have their roots in the Ayurvedic tradition. But there is so much more great wisdom in Ayurveda that you can take advantage of, and it's my feeling that even a rudimentary understanding of Ayurveda's principles can help you begin to change your life in simple and commonsense ways that can have lasting benefits for your health.

The purpose of this book is to give you a sense of Ayurveda's scope and provide you with a basic and easy-to-understand foundation. You can use this book to familiarize yourself with some of the concepts of Ayurveda, and you can try out some of the practices that are described. Once you have oriented yourself, you may wish to explore further, and many resources are listed in the back.

one

AYURVEDA,
THE SCIENCE OF LONG LIFE

The word *Ayurveda* can be broken down to its roots: *ayur,* which means "life," and *veda,* which means "knowledge." It is most commonly translated as "the science of life" or, more specifically, "the science of long life."

This ancient Indian system of healing has evolved over many centuries and is believed to be 5,000 years old and possibly older. It is still practiced in India today, and for many Indians, its simpler folk remedies are a normal part of growing up. In the West, in the last fifteen years or so, there has been a wave of new interest in Ayurveda. What Westerners are realizing as they explore Ayurveda is that, while some of the principles and practices may at first seem foreign, the system as a whole makes sense. More important, it works, and people are discovering that Ayurveda has a great deal to offer the modern Western person.

This new interest has partly to do with the sudden and widespread popularity of one of Ayurveda's sister sciences, yoga, which comes out of the same Vedic tradition. Ayurveda and yoga evolved simultaneously and are complementary systems. David Frawley, a scholar of both systems, describes Ayurveda as the healing branch of yogic science, while yoga is the spiritual aspect of Ayurveda. Many people come to Ayurveda through their practice of yoga, but the opposite is true as well. The point is that the two systems are meant to work together.

The idea is to create such abundant health through Ayurveda that we begin to open more and more to the spiritual aspect of our being. The flowering of our health allows and supports us to be more directly in touch with our spirit—our innate intelligence, or wisdom—and to live more consistently out of that growing awareness. This is the path of yoga, and its final aim is liberation, or Self-realization. Self-realization is said to be an ecstatic state that is quite beyond anything we have previously experienced.

Ayurveda's primary methods for healing are natural: instead of relying on synthetic drugs for quick fixes, Ayurveda mostly uses food, herbs, and gentle lifestyle practices like yoga, breathing exercises, and meditation to cultivate optimal health. Other adjunct therapies that are sometimes used include *mantra* (chant), massage therapy, self-massage, aromatherapy, gem therapy, and metal and mineral therapies. Through the use of these natural, noninvasive methods, the total health of your being is built up slowly and steadily.

Ayurveda is nature-based in another sense as well. Each person is seen as part of an even greater whole: we exist not in some void by ourselves, but within the natural world. This world has certain irrefutable laws and patterns that regulate all that exists: we see this every day in the simple rising and setting of the sun. As creatures that are part of this natural order, we also are subject to the laws of nature—the laws of our own *human* nature. It makes sense that if we live according to these laws, we have a much better chance of surviving and enjoying a healthy life. If, on the other hand, we don't align ourselves with these laws, then disease, disharmony, and unhappiness result.

For example, suppose you are the kind of person who happens to need a fair amount of sleep, but you keep staying up late. Then, because you have to get up early in the morning to go to work, you end up drinking lots of coffee during the day to stay awake. The coffee actually gives you indigestion, and over time you start having stomach problems. Because your stomach is bothering you, you can't manage to get to bed at a reasonable hour. In this way, an unhealthy cycle gets set up, which could have been avoided entirely if there had been some recognition of your natural need for more sleep. This is a simple example, but it illustrates how Ayurveda's purpose is to realign us with our own nature.

Ayurveda has a highly developed theoretical side that explains the workings of the universe and how we as human beings fit into that. To fully grasp this view, one must become familiar with Indian philosophy, and this can take many years of study. Luckily, Ayurveda is also amazingly practical and accessible, and it offers a precise and profound understanding of human nature that includes many specific suggestions and guidelines to live by.

BODY, MIND, AND SPIRIT

In Western medicine, there is a tendency to identify and treat physical symptoms without necessarily probing into their origin. By contrast, Ayurveda looks at the whole person in order to gain a deep understanding of the presenting symptoms.

Suppose, for example, that you go to a typical Western doctor because you're feeling sick. You will likely be given a prescription for a drug that will effectively suppress your symptoms but won't actually address the root causes of your illness. An Ayurvedic practitioner, on the other hand, will be interested in looking at all dimensions of your being to see what might have made you vulnerable to getting sick in the first place. Your overall physical health will be considered thoroughly, but so will the mental and spiritual aspects of your being. What was your mental state before you got sick, and what are your general mental tendencies most of the time? Are you in a happy place in your life right now? In Ayurveda, it doesn't make sense to try to heal the body without taking into account a person's mental and spiritual condition. Body, mind, and spirit are seen as inextricably intertwined, so any kind of treatment or lifestyle recommendations that are made have to take into account these three aspects. Deepak Chopra writes in *Perfect Balance,* "The guiding principle of Ayurveda is that the mind exerts the deepest influence on the body, and freedom from sickness depends upon contacting our own awareness, bringing it into balance, and then extending that balance to the body."

Ayurveda also takes into account the larger context of your life. After all, you can't really look at these three dimensions of yourself—body, mind, and spirit—without giving some thought to the exterior things that will influence those parts of you. So Ayurveda considers factors like the weather and the seasons and how these may affect you. Ayurveda also looks at the food that you are putting into your body, the kinds of activities that you are engaged in, the work you do, and the relationships you're involved in. *Every* aspect of daily life is factored into the assessment of your health and the treatments and lifestyle recommendations that are then prescribed.

Ayurveda has treatments for all different sorts of health problems, from more mild conditions like common colds to those that are quite severe and even life-threatening. The thrust of Ayurveda, though, is to try to *prevent* disease from occurring in the first place.

In order to stay healthy, you need to be an active participant in your health management. This means that while you may receive prescriptions and lifestyle recommendations from an Ayurvedic practitioner, it is ultimately up to you to take responsibility for integrating these into your life. In this way, you are empowered to actively participate in your own healing instead of just relying on someone else to cure you. With this approach, you'll be able to attain and maintain a whole new level of vibrant health.

Part of what makes it possible to monitor your own health is understanding your unique constitution. Ayurveda has long recognized how much human beings can vary from one another. Some people have fast metabolisms and need to eat frequently and regularly; others can easily skip meals without even noticing. Some people feel at ease in a hot climate, while others are totally enervated. Some can stay up all night and hardly feel it, while for others this would create exhaustion the next day. There are light sleepers, and there are people who can barely be roused in the morning. The list could go on and on. The point is that the same weather, foods, activities, and lifestyle choices do not have the same effect on everyone: we are unique beings, with our own special physical and mental tendencies. While we are unique, Ayurveda also recognizes that certain patterns are common; hence, a clever system of classifying people by their type, or constitution, is used.

Understanding what your type is puts you in a much better position to make sensible, health-promoting choices. As you understand more about your type, or *dosha,* as it's called, you'll have a better sense of what foods are good for you, how much sleep you need, what sort of exercise is likely to be most beneficial, and many other things. Even subtle changes in your life can, over time, have a profound impact on your state of health. In addition to the physical benefits, you may experience the mental relief that comes with seeing yourself more clearly; instead of trying to be something you aren't, you may recognize that "this is just the way I am, and it simply means that I need to do this as opposed to that." Knowledge of your own dosha may make you curious about other people, too, eager to understand them according to this system, and these insights can help bring harmony to your relationships. In the next chapter, you'll find more information about the doshas as well as questionnaires to help you determine your dosha.

AYURVEDA'S ROOTS

The exact origins of Ayurveda are unknown, but it is clear that it began somewhere in ancient India, long before Christ's time or even the Buddha's. It was originally an oral tradition, passed along by enlightened seers, or *rishis,* who had closely observed nature and were able to ascertain certain fundamental laws and how they related to human beings.

The earliest written records of Ayurveda are contained in the Vedas, or Vedic hymns, which make up the oldest and largest body of sacred knowledge in human history. (The Vedas were written somewhere between 2000 and 4000 B.C.E., and they consist of 20,358 verses!) Ayurveda's first appearance is in the last and youngest of the Vedas, known as *Atharva Veda;* according to scholar Georg Feuerstein, this text consists of about 6,000 verses and 1,000 lines in prose, "most of which deal with magic spells and charms designed to either promote peace, health, love, and material or spiritual prosperity, or to call down disaster on an enemy."

How Ayurveda further developed is not exactly clear, but a later medical text that emerged is called the *Charaka-Samhita. Charaka* refers to the author; *Samhita* translates as "compendium." This text is the most famous of all the ancient Ayurvedic texts; it is full of theory and philosophy, but it also describes, among other things, the cellular structure of the body and includes lists of microscopic organisms that may cause disease.

Another well-known medical text is the *Sushruta-Samhita,* believed to have been authored by the physician Sushruta, who may have lived in the sixth century B.C.E. and was possibly a contemporary of the Buddha. The *Sushruta-Samhita* contains information on surgical methods and equipment; along with detailed medical information, it also includes philosophical and spiritual advice on how to live a healthy life. (An interesting point to know about the *Sushruta-Samhita* is that it contains details of an operation on noses and ears that is still famous today. Surgeons throughout the world continue to think of Sushruta as the founder of plastic surgery.) Other texts came later, including the *Ashtanga Hridaya of Vagbhata,* which is said to have been written around 700 C.E. and is the most widely used Ayurvedic text today.

Over the centuries, Ayurveda spread into many other parts of the world; traces of it are evident in traditional medical systems of China, Nepal, and Tibet, and it even traveled as far east as Indonesia. We also know that Alexander the Great's invasion of India in the fourth century B.C.E. led to a certain amount of overlap between Greek and Indian cultures, and Ayurveda eventually penetrated into Greece itself, where it influenced the development of medicine there.

Many years later, during the fifteenth century, European colonization of India began. India did not fare well under the thumb of the nations that variously ruled during the following centuries; many atrocities were committed against Indians, and much of Indian culture was suppressed. By the early nineteenth century, when the British reigned, Ayurveda had no official support; in fact, in 1835 the British banned the practice of Ayurveda in favor of European medicine in those regions where the East

India Company ruled. From this point on, Ayurveda was practiced mostly in rural areas. Then, at the beginning of the twentieth century, those in favor of Indian independence began arguing for the restoration and proper recognition of Ayurveda, and eventually, after 1947, this movement bore fruit.

Today, Ayurveda is taught in a number of reputable schools and universities in India, and there seems to be a stronger resurgence of interest in this ancient science, even in India. In the West, during the eighties, many people began to learn about Ayurveda through Maharishi Mahesh Yogi, the founder of the Transcendental Meditation movement. Since then, Deepak Chopra has been instrumental in educating people about Ayurveda. Several other doctors and scholars have emerged, both from the East and West, some of the most influential being Vasant Lad, David Frawley, and Robert Svoboda. These people and many others have done a great deal to help interpret the ancient teachings of Ayurveda in a way that makes sense to Westerners.

Ayurveda is a deep science, and it is just as relevant today as it was four or five thousand years ago—perhaps even more so! This is an exciting time to be living in, as the wisdom of this tradition is brought forth again and made available to interested people.

two

LIVING IN TUNE WITH YOUR NATURE
Discovering Your Constitution

Ayurveda explains that all of nature is made up of five ele-ments: space, air, fire, water, and earth. When these elements are charged with the life-force, or *prana*, they combine to form the three doshas. Space and air combine to form the *Vata* dosha; fire and water together create the *Pitta* dosha; and water and earth combine to make the *Kapha* dosha. These three building blocks are in everything that exists, including, of course, humans.

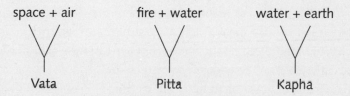

Our existence is a kind of play among these three forces, and the balance among the doshas is what determines our state of health. It is as simple as this: when the doshas are in their ideal, balanced state, we feel strong, our organs function properly, our complexion is healthy, and we experience a sense of well-being. When any one of the doshas is out of balance or in an aggravated state, then our systems go awry in any number of ways.

It is said that our constitution is determined at the moment we are conceived; this original constitution is known as *prakruti*. It is decided both by the dominant dosha of the moment itself—the season you are born in and the time of day—and by the dominant doshas of the parents. Thus, a person born of parents who have Kapha dominant in their constitutions will likely have Kapha dominance, too. The constitution that we are born with stays with us for our lifetime. We remain healthy when we can learn to regulate the dosha that tends to dominate and to go out of balance.

Each of the doshas controls different aspects of our being, and each locates itself in particular areas of the body. Each of us has all of the doshas within, but usually one dosha is predominant. This simply means that a person has more traits associated with one dosha over another. It also means that a person will have more of a tendency toward imbalance in that particular dosha. However, it's important to note that while one dosha may be more prone to imbalance, it is still possible for the other doshas to become unbalanced as well.

A note about terminology: the words *dosha, type,* and *constitution* are used interchangeably. Also, when we speak about a person's dominant dosha, we usually refer to that person as *being* his or her dosha; in other words, we might say, "Jane is a Vata," or "Jane is a Vata type," or even, simply, "Jane is Vata." In addition, it is common to talk both about the qualities of the dosha itself and about what happens to a person when a dosha gets out of balance. Finally, when we talk about a dosha going out of balance, we may alternatively describe it as being aggravated, increased, or in excess. This fluid use of terminology will become obvious and make more sense to you as you read on.

VATA

The Vata dosha can be described as the force that allows for all movements within the body. These include circulation of breath and blood; menstruation; and the passage of food through the digestive tract and out the body. Vata is the dosha that controls the entire nervous system; it is also what moves the other two doshas. Vata resides primarily in the colon, and when Vata is out of balance, a physical symptom can be excessive gas. Aggravated Vata can create psychosomatic disturbances, too, giving rise to emotions like fear, anxiety, and worry. It is considered the most important dosha and is often the most out of balance of all the doshas, leading to the greatest number of diseases and conditions.

PITTA

Pitta comes from the Sanskrit word meaning "to heat" or "to cook." It is the transformative force within us; it is what allows things to be converted or metabolized. Thus, Pitta is in charge of the biochemistry of the body, including hormones and all digestive processes. Just as Pitta helps us digest the food we put into our bodies, it also governs the digestion of thoughts, ideas, emotions, and experiences. Pitta powers our intellect and helps us make sense of our life experiences so that we can use these to grow mentally and spiritually.

Pitta is located in the small intestine and stomach. When Pitta is out of balance, it accumulates in the small intestine and creates acidity. Emotionally, excessive Pitta can cause irritability, impatience, and anger.

KAPHA

Kapha can be translated as "to keep together"; it is the force of cohesion. Being made up of water and earth elements, it is considered the most stable of the doshas. Kapha is responsible for the creation and strength of all structures in the living body, including bones, muscles, tissue, and fat.

Kapha resides in many places: in the stomach, chest, throat, and head, where it produces mucus; it is also in lymph and plasma. Kapha keeps the body lubricated, and it is what makes us emotional beings. In particular, Kapha relates to the emotion of love, and it gives us the capacity to be constant and faithful. When Kapha is thrown out of balance, it can cause lung problems, excessive weight gain, and water retention. Negative emotions that can arise are depression, lethargy, greed, and possessiveness.

DETERMINING YOUR DOSHA

By now you are probably curious to know what dosha predominates in your constitution. At the end of this section, you will find a questionnaire that will help you determine your type. Below are more in-depth descriptions of each of the doshas, starting with the physical characteristics and then examining the mental tendencies. As you read these, you will probably find that you relate to one dosha more than the others. However, it's quite possible that aspects of two doshas will ring true for you; this is, in fact, fairly common. If you find yourself relating to two, you'll likely notice that one of them is a bit stronger than the other. In rare instances, a person will have equal proportions of all three doshas. What this means, in effect, is that your constitution could be described by one of ten possibilities. They are:

Vata	Pitta	Kapha	Vata-Pitta-Kapha
Vata-Pitta	Pitta-Vata	Kapha-Vata	
Vata-Kapha	Pitta-Kapha	Kapha-Pitta	

In a Vata-Pitta combination, Vata is a bit more dominant than Pitta, while in the Pitta-Vata combination, Pitta is stronger than Vata, and so on. Also, to complicate things still further, sometimes people have physical characteristics of one dosha, while their mental tendencies come from another dosha. The Vata-Pitta-Kapha combination is very unusual and is said to be the best, most innately balanced type.

VATA

Physical Characteristics

Vata people are the leanest of the doshas: they tend to have small bones and underweight, flexible bodies. They are either quite short or very tall, and they usually have a hard time putting on weight. One of the main qualities of Vata dosha is dryness, and so Vata people tend to have dry skin that wrinkles easily. Lips and tongue can be dry as well, and sometimes there is a tendency to get hoarse. This same dryness can cause constipation; it can also cause cracking in the joints. Coarseness is another quality that can show up in cracked skin, split ends of hair, and nails that break easily. The hair is usually dark, thin, and brittle.

Vatas are characterized by irregularity: a Vata person's face can be asymmetrical, with an uneven nose or large, uneven ears. Their eyes, which are small and dark, tend to move around nervously; their heartbeat can be irregular; and they can suffer from tremors and nervous tics. Teeth are large, broken, or uneven. Eating, drinking, and sleeping habits are often erratic; digestion is not so reliable, and there can be a tendency to get gas. Vatas have poor stamina and don't cope well with intense physical challenge or stress. Though they have a strong interest in initiating sex, they are usually quickly sated.

Vata people are frequently cold; they hardly sweat; and their circulation is poor, causing them to have cold hands and feet. As a result, heat is very appealing to Vatas.

Just as wind moves, Vata people like to be on the move, too, and they do many things quickly, often on impulse. They eat quickly, walk quickly, and talk quickly; when they're unbalanced, their speech can be unclear. Even though they have poor stamina, they are drawn to fast and vigorous exercise, like jogging, but these sorts of activities actually aggravate their Vata condition rather than balance it.

Some typical Vata ailments include headaches, earaches, sore and dry throats, constipation, gas, and arthritis.

Mental Characteristics

When they are in balance, Vatas are blessed with plenty of creative energy and imagination; they are visionary people and often choose careers in the arts. Sometimes Vatas have a mental clarity that actually translates into clairvoyance.

A balanced Vata person is happy and loving and able to respond immediately and with enthusiasm. Vatas have quick, fluid minds, and they can learn and grasp things easily. They generally earn money easily, and one of the ways they are inclined to spend it is by traveling.

Though Vatas learn readily, when they are out of balance, they can just as quickly forget what they've learned. An unbalanced Vata's thinking can become hyperactive and unclear. Taken still further, Vatas can become spacey, anxious, and fearful.

They may be good at earning money, but Vatas aren't necessarily able to hold onto it. They can be terribly restless, which can translate into a compulsion to change anything and everything in their lives. Their love of travel can also make it difficult for them to maintain any kind of stability. They can have a hard time with commitment and are notorious for changing jobs, houses, and relationships.

Janice, who is a writer and the owner of a beautiful art gallery, is a good example of a typical Vata person. In addition to running her art gallery, Janice teaches creative writing classes. When she is in a healthy, balanced state, she has plenty of energy and enthusiasm for her work, and she is widely available to a large community of students and art lovers who are very fond of her. She has a lively and loving disposition and a wonderful sense of humor. Naturally curious, she is interested in many things of the world, and she must take at least one long trip abroad every year.

Physically, Janice tends toward dryness; she needs plenty of water to keep her system adequately hydrated, and she can tend toward constipation if she doesn't drink enough. She does not like the wind, and she usually wears silk undershirts to keep the core of her body warm. She is sensitive to sound and dislikes extraneous noise.

Janice can get carried away in the moment and, in her enthusiasm, extend herself far beyond what is really sustainable for her body type. Sometimes she stays up into the late hours of the night reading or watching television, only to wake up exhausted the next day. She occasionally forgets to eat, and then when it dawns on her that she is hungry, she may overeat or make bad food choices by, for example, eating lamb or beef (which are not recommended for Vata types). When she is out of balance, she can be absentminded and spacey. It is challenging for her to complete projects, though she has many brilliant ideas. She realizes that routines are very grounding and beneficial, but she has difficulty establishing these and sticking with them in a regular way. When she feels overwhelmed by the demands of her work, she can become fearful and panicky.

Summary of Vata Characteristics

- Thin, light, delicate physique; either very tall or very short
- Tendency toward dryness: dry hair, skin, lips; constipation
- Tendency toward roughness: rough skin, hair, nails, hands, and feet
- Cracking or unstable joints
- Stiff muscles
- Sensitive to cold: dislikes cold climates
- Cold extremities, poor circulation
- Prone to palpitations, irregular heartbeat, muscle spasms, nervous stomach
- Tremors and tics
- Changeable moods; irregular daily habits
- Irregular appetite; irregular digestion; prone to gas
- Sensitive to wind and sound
- Prone to sore throats, earaches, dry coughs, headaches, anxiety
- Low physical endurance; tends to overexert
- Energy comes in brief, sudden bursts
- Ready interest in sex; quick to be sated
- Likes travel

- Light sleeper, sometimes insomniac; many dreams that are active and quick moving

- Highly imaginative and creative

- Enthusiastic, excitable, and positive when in balance

- Mentally quick but forgets easily

- Can't save money easily

Balancing Vata

Here are a few basic guidelines that you can follow to help you balance Vata. Avoid cold temperatures, and make sure to keep warm, especially in the winter. Stay away from cold and raw foods, and eat more warm and spicy foods. Try to avoid excess stimulation, and don't overexert yourself. As much as you can, get regular and adequate rest. Try to create routines and stick to them.

PITTA

Physical Characteristics

Pitta people are usually an average height and weight, though some of them can be on the slim side. Their weight tends to stay about the same; their muscles are average; and they are generally the most physically balanced of all the doshas. They have better stamina and endurance than Vata types, though not as much as Kaphas do.

Pittas have light, bright eyes—often green, gray, or blue—and their eyes are a medium size, with a penetrating, sharp quality. This same sharpness can be seen in certain features, like the nose, chin, or teeth. Pitta's skin is oily; it is sensitive and burns easily; and often it is flushed or freckled. When out of balance, Pittas are prone to skin problems like rashes, acne, or inflammation. They have silky, reddish hair, and they typically lose their hair or go gray prematurely.

Unlike Vatas, Pittas are usually quite warm, and as a result, they have very little tolerance for heat. This makes it difficult for them to live in hot climates, be in the sun, or do hard, physical labor when the temperature is hot. They sweat a great deal, and their sweat can have a noticeably strong odor.

Pitta types have fast metabolisms; their appetite is strong and can come on suddenly. They need to eat frequently or else risk getting irritable and out of sorts. They are capable of consuming a lot of food and drink; their digestion is strong and reliable; and they produce a great deal of urine and feces.

When Pitta is aggravated, typical problems that arise are ulcers, heartburn, stomach acidity, insomnia, vision problems, and inflammations of the skin like acne, boils, or rashes.

Mental Characteristics

Pittas have sharp, logical minds, with good powers of concentration. They are focused and orderly in their thinking, and they can make good, charismatic speakers. They are confident and enjoy a good challenge. They like and need to have something—a difficult problem or project, for example—to focus their attention and energy on. They are generally very bright people who excel at whatever they choose to do. They like to be in control, and they can make excellent managers and leaders.

When out of balance, their fiery nature becomes too dominant, and they are prone to impatience, irritability, and anger. They can become overly opinionated, sarcastic, competitive, and domineering. They can be perfectionistic and overly meticulous. At their worst, they can be stubborn and fanatical. They tend to burn themselves out through too much thinking, aggressive behavior, and constant striving.

Stacey, who is Pitta type, is a highly successful entrepreneur based in New York. In her late twenties she single-handedly started a magazine, which is now widely read and very well respected in literary and academic circles. She is ambitious, hardworking, and resourceful; she likes the status that her position affords; and she usually knows exactly what she wants and wastes no time waffling over decisions. Her environment is important to her, and she is willing to spend money to make her home and office beautiful and inviting.

Stacey has a mane of flaming red hair, which, as she gets older, is thinning slightly. Her green eyes are medium sized, and she has an intimidating, penetrating stare. Her build is average, and her weight does not fluctuate. She tends to be hot and sweaty, and a tropical island is about the last place she'd want to go to for a vacation. Usually, her digestion is good, and she has a strong appetite; if she doesn't eat as soon as she feels hungry, her mood turns foul.

When she is in a healthy, balanced state, she is charming, witty, and articulate. She is very focused and accomplishes a great deal. She is, however, extremely perfectionistic and has no patience for what she sees as mediocrity, either in herself or others. When she is under stress, her temper can flare, alienating many people. Her employees generally don't last long, as the combined stress of her domineering personality and micromanaging style can be overwhelming.

Summary of Pitta Characteristics

- Medium body size; steady weight

- Hot body temperature; dislikes heat

- Light-colored eyes: usually gray, green, hazel, or blue; sharp gaze

- Red or light-colored hair; grays or goes bald prematurely

- Fair, freckled, or red skin that burns easily

- Oily skin and hair

- Prone to acne, rashes, or inflammation

- Good digestion; loose stools

- Strong, urgent appetite
- Dislikes oily food
- Sensitive to light
- Eyes are sensitive and easily irritated
- Abundant energy
- Sharp memory
- Prone to heartburn, stomach acidity
- Profuse sweat, urine, feces
- Strong body odor: smelly feet, armpits, mouth
- Prone to anger and impatience; judgmental and critical
- Hardworking and successful
- Earns good money but spends it, too

Balancing Pitta

Here are a few basic guidelines that you can follow to help you balance Pitta. Avoid hot temperatures when you can; keep cool, especially in the summer. Stay away from hot or spicy foods, as well as grease, oil, and salt. Eat cool foods and drink cool beverages. Make sure to get adequate exercise that doesn't involve competition or comparison. Try to have something positive to focus your energy on.

Physical Characteristics

Kaphas have strong, sturdy, and well-developed bodies. Their bones tend to be large, and they carry more weight on their frames than Vata or Pitta types. When they are in balance, they have the most energy of all of the types, and they have strong immune systems. They have a great deal of capacity for intense physical activity; this translates into their sexual lives as well, where they are slow to be aroused but can continue for long periods of time.

Because they are ruled by the earth and water elements, Kaphas can have a tendency toward weight gain—even obesity— and fluid retention; these tendencies are made worse by the fact that Kaphas have a slow metabolism and digestion. Unlike Vatas and Pitta, Kaphas can easily skip meals with no ill effects.

Kaphas tend to run cool and prefer to avoid cold, damp conditions: they do better in windy or sunny places. Their skin can be cool as well as oily, moist, and thick. One of the Kapha qualities is softness, so Kapha people often have soft skin and hair as well as a soft voice. Their eyes tend to be dark and large, with a gentle expression. They may have long, thick eyelashes and eyebrows, and the hair on the rest of their bodies can be thick and abundant.

Since Kapha people are the most stable of all the types, they generally do everything without hurrying; their movements and speech may be quite slow; their digestion is slow; and they evacuate slowly, too. Their sleep is deep and long, and it takes them awhile to wake up in the morning; they usually need coffee, or some stimulant, to fully wake up.

Physical problems that arise when Kapha is aggravated include colds, flus, sinus headaches, congestion, and various respiratory problems, including asthma, hay fever, and allergies. More extreme conditions associated with this type are diabetes and heart attack.

Mental Characteristics

Kaphas are usually very loving, affectionate, and tolerant. They are faithful and reliable, and when they are happy and balanced, they are easygoing, undemanding, and forgiving.

Kaphas are unhurried and steady in all they do: they make decisions slowly and are slow to get going on activities. They can take awhile to grasp new ideas and information, though once they have learned something, they usually don't forget it. In general, their memories are good.

When Kaphas put their minds to something, their innate steadfastness and energy usually pay off. They are good, not just at earning money, but also holding onto it. Comfort and security are important to them.

When they are unbalanced, Kaphas can become greedy and possessive. Though they are blessed with inherently strong bodies, they dislike exercise and try to avoid it. This tendency toward sloth can lead to lethargy and depression, particularly when it's coupled with a love of food. In more extreme cases, an unbalanced Kapha may become obese. Kaphas can have a hard time communicating their feelings, and, rather than rock the boat, they may suppress their emotions (at times using food to achieve this) in order to maintain peace and harmony.

Sanjay has many of the traits of a Kapha person. Sanjay has been in banking for all of his working life, which amounts to more than ten years. Over time, he has moved up in the ranks to a senior management position. His peers respect him, and he is well liked as a manager for his open-minded, hands-off style.

Sanjay is a big man. He has a tendency toward plumpness and usually carries a little extra fat around his middle, which tends to expand when he neglects his exercise or indulges in a few too many rich meals. His hair is curly and covers his body; his skin is soft and smooth. He has enormous eyes, with long, lustrous eyelashes and thick eyebrows.

Sanjay likes his creature comforts. Home is important to him, and he needs a large, well-built house equipped with all of the usual conveniences. He likes driving a good car and taking vacations in warm, sunny climes; and he is somewhat of a gourmand who enjoys eating out at finer restaurants. Sanjay is very affectionate and loves to cuddle in bed. He is extremely attached to his sleep, and it is impossible to rouse him in the morning before he is ready. He takes several hours to wake up fully, and a cup of strong coffee is a daily requirement.

Sanjay is rarely upset by anything; he is quite even-tempered and explodes only occasionally, if really pushed. Most of the time he is healthy, but his sedentary work and travel schedule can make him prone to chest colds and congestion. He is mildly allergic to certain foods, plants, and dust, and he suffers an occasional asthma attack.

Summary of Kapha Characteristics

- Large, well-built frame; tendency to be overweight
- Sensitive to cold and damp; likes sun and wind
- Large eyes
- Smooth, soft skin
- Sensitive to touch
- Soft, wavy hair; hair all over
- Strong immunity when in balance
- Reliable energy; strong physical stamina
- Slow metabolism and digestion
- Slow and steady in most activities; stable, easygoing, reliable
- Slow learner, but retains information once it's learned
- Slow to anger; avoids conflict; tries to maintain peace
- Loving, affectionate, kind, gentle, and forgiving: highly tolerant

- Difficulty expressing emotions; may stuff emotions using food

- Loves food, especially sweets

- Loves sleep

- Prone to problems involving mucus production: colds, flus, nasal congestion

- Prone to asthma and allergies; diabetes and heart attack

- Prone to depression, grief, possessiveness, greed

Balancing Kapha

To balance Kapha, try to observe these basic guidelines. Make sure to stay warm and dry. Avoid heavy, sweet, fatty, or oily foods as well as dairy and cold drinks. Eat foods that are lighter, and don't overeat or snack. Try not to oversleep, and make sure to get plenty of vigorous exercise

DETERMINING YOUR TYPE

Below are two questionnaires that are meant to help clarify your type. The first questionnaire focuses on physical attributes, while the second examines mental and emotional tendencies. As you proceed, try to be objective and honest. Remember that this is not about how you'd like to be but how you actually are. Check off what is true for you *most of the time*, even if you are experiencing something different right at the moment. Sometimes going with your first response is best. If at some point you feel completely stuck, just skip that part and move on to the next. Occasionally, you may find that two answers apply equally, in which case you can check both. To confirm the accuracy of your responses, you may want to have someone close to you look at your self-assessment and give you feedback.

Place a check next to the choice that best describes you. When you are done, total the number of checks in each category to determine your physical type.

VATA	PITTA	KAPHA
___ Thin; unusually short or tall	___ Medium height; average frame	___ Large, stout frame; usually short, but sometimes tall and large
___ Low weight; doesn't gain weight easily	___ Medium weight; stays about the same weight	___ Heavy weight; easy to gain weight, hard to lose
___ Small, dark eyes, that tend to move around	___ Medium-sized, light eyes (green, blue, gray, hazel); piercing gaze; eyes are easily inflamed	___ Large eyes, with thick eyelashes; soft, gentle gaze

VATA	PITTA	KAPHA
___ Dry, rough, cold skin; chaps or cracks easily	___ Moist, warm, freckled, or pink skin; prone to inflammations like acne	___ Soft, smooth, moist, and cool skin
___ Darker complexion; tans without burning	___ Flushed complexion; sunburns easily	___ Pale complexion; tans evenly without burning
___ Rough, dry, wiry hair	___ Thin, oily, light-colored hair; grays or balds prematurely	___ Thick, wavy, oily hair
___ Thin, small eyebrows	___ Medium eyebrows	___ Thick, bushy eyebrows
___ Small, thin nose; uneven shape	___ Medium-sized nose; fairly symmetrical	___ Wide nose
___ Teeth vary in size; crooked	___ Medium-sized, even teeth	___ Large, white, even teeth
___ Stiff joints that tend to crack	___ Loose, average-sized joints	___ Large, sturdy joints
___ Thin, brittle nails	___ Soft, pink nails	___ Strong, thick, white, smooth nails
___ Thin, undeveloped muscles	___ Average-sized muscles	___ Large, well-developed muscles

VATA	PITTA	KAPHA
___ Scant, colorless urine	___ Profuse, yellow urine	___ Moderate, milky urine
___ Irregular, scanty menstrual flow	___ Regular menstrual flow; bright color	___ Regular menstrual flow; pale color
___ Scanty, dry, hard stools; prone to gas and constipation	___ Abundant, loose, and soft stools	___ Moderate, dense stools; can have mucus in them
___ Variable appetite; needs to eat frequently	___ Strong, urgent appetite; irritable if meals are missed	___ Low appetite, but may eat out of emotional need
___ Likes to snack on dry, crunchy foods	___ Likes cold drinks and snacks	___ Likes sweets and creamy foods
___ Low thirst	___ Very thirsty	___ Moderate thirst
___ Variable digestion; prone to gas	___ Good, strong, fast digestion	___ Slow, steady digestion
___ Hardly sweats	___ Profuse, strong-smelling sweat	___ Moderate sweat
___ Poor circulation: cold hands and feet; cold temperature	___ Good circulation; temperature runs hot	___ Moderate circulation; temperature runs cool
___ Likes sun and warmth	___ Likes cooler weather	___ Likes warm and windy weather
___ Sensitive to cold, wind, dryness, noise	___ Sensitive to heat, sunlight, light, and color	___ Sensitive to touch, cold, and dampness

34

VATA	PITTA	KAPHA
___ Low immunity	___ Moderate immunity	___ Strong immunity
___ Low physical endurance; easily exhausted	___ Moderate physical endurance	___ Strong physical endurance
___ Light sleep; tends toward insomnia	___ Moderate or variable sleep	___ Deep, excessive sleep; falls asleep easily
___ Nervous disease tendencies	___ Tends toward inflammation and fever	___ Tends toward excess mucus, congestion, water retention
Total _____	Total _____	Total _____

Place a check next to the choice that best describes you. When you are done, total the number of checks in each category to determine your mental-emotional type.

VATA	PITTA	KAPHA
___ Dreams are full of movement; can be prone to nightmares	___ Colorful, vivid, passionate dreams	___ Rarely dreams; dreams are uneventful
___ Moves quickly and erratically	___ Moves with purpose and motivation	___ Moves slowly, steadily, and gracefully

VATA	PITTA	KAPHA
___Changes mind quickly and easily; indecisive and nervous	___ Is opinionated, decisive, and determined	___ Changes mind and opinions slowly; likes things as they are
___Thinks creatively; has lots of ideas and vision	___ Thinks logically, critically, and idealistically	___ Thinks slowly and methodically
___Learns easily but forgets easily; poor long-term memory	___ Learns easily and has a clear memory	___ Learns slowly but retains what's learned; good long-term memory
___Prone to anxiety, fear, nervousness, and worry	___ Prone to irritability, anger, aggression, and jealousy	___ Prone to depression, lethargy, attachment, and greed
___Lively and positive outlook when in balance	___ Warm, outgoing, and confident when in balance	___ Peaceful, happy, content, and loving when in balance
___Drawn to professions in the arts	___ Drawn to "noble" professions like law, medicine, engineering	___ Drawn to business
___Spends easily on trifles	___ Earns, but spends money on luxurious items	___ Can earn and save if motivated

VATA	PITTA	KAPHA
___Quick speech; talks a lot	___ Argumentative, confrontational; enjoys debate	___ Talks slowly and deliberately
___ Loves travel	___ Needs a beautiful environment	___ Domestic, more of a homebody
___ Sensitive to sound	___ Sensitive to visual stimulation	___ Sensitive to touch
___ High interest in initiating sex; quickly sated	___ Moderate to strong sexual drive	___ Slow to be aroused; lasts for a long time
___ Rebellious, independent	___ Likes to take the lead	___ Loyal and dependable
Total _____	Total _____	Total _____

Interpreting Your Scores

Once you have totaled your scores, these numbers will give you an idea of what your type is. You may find that your constitution is clearly dominated by one or another dosha. Sometimes one dosha comes out a little bit ahead, followed fairly closely by another. You may also find that while you have the physical characteristics of one dosha, your mental and emotional makeup is dominated more by a different dosha. In both of these instances, it is quite likely that your constitution is ruled by two doshas; the majority of people, are, in fact, a combination.

If you feel confused about your dosha, remember that these questionnaires may give you only a general idea; to be accurately assessed, you need to consult with an Ayurvedic practitioner who will be able to draw on other tools.

three

LAYING THE FOUNDATION FOR HEALTH
Eating for Your Constitution

Since you now know what your type is, you are naturally interested in how you can apply this information to your life. One of the fundamental aspects of an Ayurvedic lifestyle involves proper eating. This chapter begins by explaining some of the theory behind Ayurvedic eating and then goes into more detail about how to use foods—both as prevention and for healing—to create optimal health.

Ayurveda places a great deal of importance on food; this is because food is the thing that you most consistently consume. Food is actually seen as medicine; it can support your health, or it can detract from it. This is not hard to believe, as you've probably had experiences of particular foods making you feel physically robust, while others leave you feeling unwell.

You may have noticed, too, that food can influence your state of mind. Some foods are described as being *rajasic,* meaning that they have more of a stimulating effect on your mind. Others are *tamasic* and produce a sedating, or dulling, effect.

There are also foods that are *sattvic* and create a sense of mental clarity and balance, which is the ideal. We won't go into further details about these food properties in this book, but you can, on your own, make a point of beginning to attune yourself to the effects of food on your mental state.

FOOD AND THE DOSHAS

You may have observed that some people can easily eat certain foods, while other people are made sick by these same things. Ayurveda has long recognized that the same foods affect people in different ways. This happens because a dosha is increased or aggravated by foods that have *similar* properties to the dosha. So, for instance, if you are a Kapha type, you will tend to be set out of balance by foods that have Kapha qualities, like moisture and heaviness. This means that you will probably do better staying away from rich, creamy foods and heavy meats. These very same foods, however, may be beneficial to a Vata person!

If you are a Pitta type, then you will have a greater chance of being aggravated by foods that have fiery, heating qualities, like spices, alcohol, citrus, or fermented foods. If you are a Vata person, dry or cold foods like salad and dried fruit may increase your innate tendency to be cold and dry. This phenomenon is described by the principle of "like increases like."

When imbalance occurs in the doshas, and when this is allowed to go unchecked, it can be the first step toward disease. Thus, it is important to work toward creating and maintaining balance through consuming the right foods. The concept is fairly simple: just as a dosha can be aggravated by foods that have similar qualities to the dosha, it can also be balanced by those foods that have *opposite* qualities. This means that a person with Vata imbalance should emphasize warming, moist foods; these might include things like hot cereal or warm, creamy soups. A person with Pitta imbalance will want to eat cooling foods, like salads and cold drinks. A person with Kapha imbalance should have more light, dry, and warming foods, like dried fruits, most beans, and spices.

DIGESTION

In addition to eating the right foods for your type, you also want to be sure that your digestion is functioning optimally. When your digestive fire, or *agni,* as it is known, is strong, then you will be able to easily digest and absorb many foods, and the impurities from these foods will easily be expelled from your body. However, if your doshas are out of balance, then your agni will be weakened, and you won't be able to digest your food properly.

When food doesn't get digested properly, it hangs around in its unabsorbed state and can accumulate in the gastrointestinal tract. This accumulated food turns into what is called *ama,* which author Vasant Lad describes as "a sticky, foul-smelling substance." If ama becomes excessive, then it will begin to seep and spread into other parts of the body through various channels like capillaries, blood vessels, and the lymphatic system. Lad explains that ama then clogs the channels, and the life-force, or prana, of the body is no longer able to flow properly. This eventually results in disease, which, depending on the amount of ama in the system and how long it has been building up, can be more or less serious.

The point is, then, to try to keep this accumulation of toxins from happening in the first place. Many things can help or hinder the digestive process. The quality of the food you eat is critical, and if you are regularly eating fast food like hamburgers, fries, and shakes, you are on a sure track to ama accumulation. It is important to steer clear of stale food, highly processed food, and foods that have additives or preservatives in them. Also, food eaten in the wrong combinations can cause poor digestion, as can eating late at night or on the run. It is also best not to eat when you are in a state of emotional upset. Finally, one of the worst things to do with food is to eat too much of it; when you do so, you overwork your system, and it is said that you ultimately end up shortening your life!

In addition to the above considerations, it is also helpful to keep seasonal changes in mind. The doshas, which regulate everything in the cosmos, also control the seasons, and as the seasons change, the dominant dosha in your immediate environment changes.

In the springtime, from approximately March to May, the Kapha dosha increases. This means that health problems that arise with aggravated Kapha, like colds, flus, or congestion, may be more likely to occur during that season. Especially if you are a Kapha type and already have a tendency for Kapha aggravation, then you will want to be careful during this time to eat a Kapha-pacifying diet that includes more warming, drying foods. Even if you aren't a Kapha type, there is an increased risk of developing Kapha problems or symptoms during this season, and you, too, can make slight adaptations to your diet if necessary.

In the summer, from about June through September, there is an increase in Pitta. Again, if you are a Pitta type and have an innate vulnerability to Pitta problems, then you will want to have a Pitta-pacifying diet during these months. This could mean adding more cooling drinks to your diet, as well as foods like salads. If you are not a Pitta type, but you develop Pitta symptoms (such as rashes, heartburn, or ulcers) during these months, you can also make changes in your diet to tone down your Pitta imbalance.

In the fall and winter, from October to February, Vata increases. This tends to make people, especially Vata types, more prone to symptoms like constipation, sore and dry throats, and worry or anxiety. Again, a Vata-pacifying diet that eliminates drying foods and adds more warming, moistening foods may help restore balance.

Do not be dismayed if all of this seems somewhat confusing. As you read the more specific information about balancing the doshas, the pieces will begin to fall into place and it will make more sense. It is useful to remember, too, that until you have tried some of the things being described, all of it will remain theoretical; once you actually beginning testing things out for yourself, your experience will inform your understanding.

SOME THOUGHTS ON EATING
USING AYURVEDIC PRINCIPLES

One of the best ways to immerse yourself in Ayurvedic eating is to actually experiment with cooking Indian food. Some marvelous Ayurvedic cookbooks are available that offer simple, easy-to-prepare dishes and meals. One of these is the *Ayurvedic Cookbook,* by Amadea Morningstar and Urmila Desai. Another wonderful source is *Ayurveda Cooking for Self-Healing,* by Vasant Lad, with Usha Lad. However you choose to approach your food preparation, the following basic principles will be helpful:

- Eat only when hungry; drink only when thirsty.

- Give yourself adequate time to eat; eat calmly, while sitting (not standing).

- Chew your food well to stimulate digestive enzymes.

- Eat fresh foods; avoid leftovers and stale food.

- Eat simpler foods; avoid processed foods and foods with additives or preservatives.

- When you can, eat organic foods.

- Be aware that cooked foods are usually easier to digest than raw foods. (For some types, however, a certain amount of raw food can be appropriate at times.)

- Make lunch your biggest meal, as this time of day is dominated by the Pitta dosha, and digestive fire is at its peak.

- Don't eat late at night.

- Eat in pleasant surroundings, with people you like.

- Focus on the act of eating rather than on distracting yourself with watching television, reading, or other activities.

- Emphasize those foods that are appropriate for your type.

- Drink a small amount of warm water (not iced) with your food; don't drink large quantities of fluids after a meal, as this will disrupt digestion.

- Don't eat fruit or drink fruit juice with a meal.

- Avoid overeating; stop before you feel completely full.

THE SIX TASTES

How food tastes is important because taste actually affects our doshas. In Ayurveda it is recommended that each meal include all of the six tastes, because this helps keep our doshas balanced. At the same time, a meal that includes the six tastes is said to answer all of our nutritional needs: it provides the necessary mix of fat, carbohydrates, protein, and so forth. The six tastes are sweet, sour, salty, bitter, pungent, and astringent. Below are some of the foods that contain these tastes and how each taste affects the doshas.

Sweet

The sweet taste is in foods like sugar, maple syrup, and honey; it exists in bread and grains like rice and wheat, in milk, and in many fruits.

The sweet taste decreases Vata and Pitta but increases Kapha. When it is used in moderation, it is strengthening to our vital essence, or *ojas,* and helps us live longer. It promotes tissue growth and is helpful for healing broken bones. It is good for complexion, skin, and hair and can help quench thirst. When used excessively, it can cause Kapha imbalances like colds, congestion, heaviness, lethargy, and obesity.

Sour

The sour taste is found in citrus fruits, tomatoes, cheeses, sour cream, yogurt, vinegar, and fermented foods.

The sour taste decreases Vata but increases Pitta and Kapha. Used moderately, it can stimulate appetite, salivation, and digestion; it can help with elimination and reduce gas. In general, it is refreshing and enlivening to the body. When it is overused, it can create excessive thirst, heartburn, and acid indigestion. It can cause itching and burning sensations as well as skin problems like acne and eczema. It can lead to blood toxicity and a higher level of acidity in the body.

Salty

The salty taste is in sea and rock salts and seaweeds.

The salty taste decreases Vata but increases Pitta and Kapha. In moderation, it stimulates appetite and salivation and helps with digestion, absorption, and elimination. It is a laxative as well as a sedative. Excessive salt intake can contribute to wrinkling, and it can cause graying and balding. It is connected with various skin problems, like gout and acne. It also causes excess water retention.

Pungent

The pungent taste is in hot peppers, onions, garlic, radishes, and ginger.

The pungent taste decreases Kapha but increases Vata and Pitta. It stimulates the sense of smell, improves the taste of food, and, with moderate use, can act as an appetite stimulant and aid in digestion and absorption. It can help circulation, stimulate sweating, and facilitate elimination of waste and ama. It also has antibacterial properties. When it is excessively used, the pungent taste can cause burning, fainting, and fatigue. It can also cause heartburn, nausea, and diarrhea.

Bitter

The bitter taste is in leafy greens like spinach as well as in certain herbs like dandelion and turmeric. It is also in coffee.

The bitter taste decreases Pitta and Kapha but increases Vata. According to Ayurvedic practitioner and author Vasant Lad, it is the taste most lacking in the North American diet. Although it is not an appealing taste on its own, it can bring out the flavor of other tastes. When it is used in proper amounts, its detoxifying and antibacterial properties are beneficial; it is also good for relieving burning, itching, and other skin conditions. It aids in the reduction of fevers, promotes digestion, and helps cleanse the blood. In excess, it can deplete various tissues and cause weakness and dizziness.

Astringent

The astringent taste is in green beans, pomegranates, unripe bananas, cabbage, and broccoli.

The astringent taste decreases Pitta and Kapha but increases Vata. It relieves diarrhea, reduces sweating, and promotes blood clotting. It is also anti-inflammatory. In excess, it causes constipation, gas, dryness in the mouth, and slowing of circulation.

Seeing all of this graphically helps. Below is a list of the tastes with arrows indicating if they increase or decrease a dosha.

Taste	Vata	Pitta	Kapha
Sweet	↓	↓	↑
Sour	↓	↑	↑
Salty	↓	↑	↑
Pungent	↑	↑	↓
Bitter	↑	↓	↓
Astringent	↑	↓	↓

Ideally, the doshas are in a state of balance. When that is the case, our agni, the digestive fire, is strong, and we are able to digest and absorb a wide variety of foods. However, when the doshas are out of balance, then it may be helpful to emphasize foods that have a particular taste.

Suppose you are a Pitta person, and the season is fall: although you are usually more prone to Pitta problems having to do with heat—like rashes, for example—it happens that you are now having Vata symptoms, and you are feeling a bit anxious and your throat is getting sore. You will want to slightly increase your consumption of foods that have sweet, sour, and salty tastes to help the Vata in you become more balanced. Pungent, bitter, and astringent foods will tend to increase air and gas in your system and will aggravate your Vata imbalance further, so you will want to minimize these.

Suppose it is summer and you live in a very hot place, and you're sweating a lot and feeling irritable and snappy: you are suffering a Pitta imbalance, and to counter this, you will want to up your intake of sweet, bitter, and astringent foods and steer clear of foods that are sour, salty, and pungent.

Maybe it is early spring and you are having a Kapha imbalance in the form of an allergy attack accompanied by lots of congestion. What will help you is to avoid or minimize sweet, sour, and salty foods and increase your consumption of pungent, bitter, and astringent foods.

DIETARY GUIDELINES FOR THE DOSHAS

To choose the foods that are best for you, you need to know what your type is. Because many people are a combination of two types, it may not be immediately obvious to you which guidelines you should follow. See what you are intuitively drawn to and try out some of the suggestions, and then watch carefully to see how you respond. Keep in mind that this book provides fairly basic guidelines and that you can find other books with more complete lists, including information on beverages, condiments, food combining, and other things. Should you begin to research more, you'll discover that some Ayurvedic practitioners make certain suggestions that are contradicted by others! In the end, how you feel is what's most important. Give yourself some time to experiment, because it may take awhile to become more attuned to food and its different effects on you. It is also helpful to remember that Ayurveda is meant to address your unique situation, and to do this in a more complete and thorough way, you may want help from an Ayurvedic practitioner who can discuss and clarify your questions and aid you in tailoring a diet that is right for you.

Dietary Guidelines for Vata

Because Vatas are the most likely of all the types to be malnourished and weak, meals should be larger and more frequent. Also, Vatas are the most absentminded about eating, and they are the most easily set off by skipping meals, so care should be taken to eat regularly. Vatas do better eating in the company of others rather than alone. Alcohol in moderation may be all right for Vatas; caffeine is not recommended. To counter the cold, light, dry qualities of Vata, foods should be warm, heavy, and oily. Tastes to emphasize are the sweet, sour, and salty tastes.

Foods to Emphasize

Fruits: Most sweet fruits are acceptable as long as they're not dried. The best fruits are apples (if they are cooked), apricots, bananas, cherries, coconut, fresh figs and dates (not dried), grapefruit, grapes, kiwi, lemons, limes, mangoes, oranges, papaya, peaches, pineapple, plums, soaked prunes and raisins, rhubarb, and strawberries.

Vegetables: Vegetables should be unfrozen, undried, and cooked. If you are going to eat salads or raw vegetables, then eat them seasonally and use plenty of oily dressing. The best vegetables are asparagus, beets, bell peppers, carrots, cilantro, garlic, green beans, green chilies, leeks, okra, black olives, parsnip, peas, sweet potatoes, pumpkin, rutabaga, summer and winter squashes, taro root, watercress, zucchini.

Grains: Many whole grains are good, as they are heavy and easily digested. The best grains are cooked oats, various kinds of rice, seitan, sprouted wheat, and wheat. Some breads can be aggravating to Vata because of their yeast content, which can cause gas.

Beans: Beans are not the best for Vata, as they are gas producing, so you'll want to minimize their intake. Mung beans are good, and chickpeas and red lentils are all right in moderation. You can also have tofu, though it may be hard to digest.

Dairy: Most dairy is good because of its heavy, nourishing qualities. You can have butter, buttermilk, soft cheese, cottage cheese, milk, ghee (clarified butter), goat's cheese, milk, sour cream, and yogurt. Drinking milk warm is the most nourishing way to have it; be sure not to have it with your meals, as it will be hard to digest.

Meat and fish: Many meats are grounding for Vata. Chicken, turkey, and seafood are all right in moderate amounts.

Nuts and seeds: Because of their warming, moistening qualities, most nuts and seeds are good, especially if raw. They should be eaten in small quantities, though, as they are hard to digest. If they are dried, they are more likely to cause digestive difficulties.

Oils: Oil is warming and moistening and generally good for Vata, although it can be hard to digest. Sesame oil and ghee are the best to ingest.

Herbs and spices: Salt is a must, and most spices are good for Vata. Some of the best are cinnamon, mint, mustard seed, black pepper, and turmeric. Cardamom, cloves, cumin, and ginger can also be good.

Sweeteners: Sweeteners are generally good for their strengthening action, with the exception of white sugar. Maple syrup is not recommended, unless used only occasionally.

Foods to Avoid or Reduce

Fruits: Raw apples, cranberries, melons, pears, persimmons, pomegranates, watermelon, and all dry fruits.

Vegetables: Avoid all frozen, raw, or dried vegetables. You'll want to minimize your intake of cabbage-family vegetables, which tend to create gas. Because of their drying property, mushrooms are not recommended. Many vegetables are all right in moderation if they are well cooked, and especially if ghee or oil is used.

Grains: Barley, buckwheat, corn, millet, rye, quinoa. Also, be wary of granola and dried grains.

Beans: Most beans are aggravating because they are drying and cause gas.

Dairy: Most dairy is good for Vata, though ice cream is not recommended.

Meat and fish: The main meats to avoid are beef, lamb, and pork.

Nuts and seeds: Nuts and seeds are good for Vata as long as they are not eaten in excess.

Oils: Most oils are good for Vata. You may want to avoid margarine.

Herbs and spices: When used in moderation, most herbs and spices are good for helping with appetite, dispelling gas, and digesting. Very hot spices may be too stimulating or drying.

Sweeteners: White sugar is not recommended. Maple syrup may be all right occasionally.

Dietary Guidelines for Pitta
Pittas do best eating in an aesthetically pleasing environment that helps keep them calm and cool. They should also avoid

being angry when they are eating. Cool drinks (not iced) are good for Pittas. It is best to avoid deep-fried and oily foods as well as alcohol, caffeine, and fermented foods. Pittas often like meat, but salads and raw vegetables are much better for them and are usually digestible because of the stronger digestive fire that is inherent in the Pitta nature. However, during the winter, or during times of illness or low energy, it is better to have cooked vegetables. To counter the hot, oily, and sharp qualities of Pitta, foods should be cooling, somewhat drying, and mild. Tastes to emphasize are sweet, bitter, and astringent.

Foods to Emphasize

Fruits: Most fruit and fruit juices are good for Pitta because of their cooling and calming nature. Look for fruit that is sweet and ripe. Sweet apples, sweet apricots, avocados, sweet berries, sweet cherries, coconut, dates, figs, grapes, mangoes, melons, sweet oranges, pears, sweet pineapple and plums, pomegranates, prunes, and raisins are all good.

Vegetables: Most vegetables, especially if sweet and bitter, are good. These include artichoke, asparagus, broccoli, brussels sprouts, cabbage, cauliflower, celery, cilantro, cucumber, green beans, kale and other leafy greens, lettuce, mushrooms, okra, peas, sweet peppers, potatoes, pumpkin, spaghetti squash, sprouts, and zucchini.

Grains: Most whole grains are good. These include amaranth, barley, cooked oats, oat bran, pasta, wheat, and white rice.

Beans: Because of their digestive fire, Pittas are more easily able to digest beans. However, beans should not be emphasized. Chickpeas; kidney beans; mung beans; soybeans and many of their products, like tofu and tempeh; and split peas may be all right; lentils may not be so good.

Dairy: Pittas can usually handle dairy, as long as it's not sour. Unsalted butter; soft, unsalted cheese; cottage cheese; egg whites; ghee; goat's milk; milk; soft, unsalted goat's cheese; and ice cream are acceptable.

Meat and fish: Meat can increase the Pitta tendency toward anger and aggression, especially red meat, so a vegetarian diet is recommended. White chicken, freshwater fish, and white turkey can be eaten in small amounts.

Nuts and seeds: Because of their warm and oily nature, nuts and seeds are not recommended for Pittas, though they can be a good alternative to meat for their protein content. Peeled almonds and coconut are all right.

Oils: Oils are warming and are not recommended for Pittas. Some of the best oils to use are sunflower and soy; ghee and butter are also good.

Herbs and spices: Spicy foods are heating and can be one of the main causes for aggravated Pitta. The following are acceptable: cardamom, cilantro, coriander, cumin, dill, fennel, mint, saffron, and turmeric.

Sweeteners: Pittas are able to digest most sweeteners. Good sweeteners to use are barley malt, fruit juice concentrates, maple syrup, rice syrup, and turbinado.

Foods to Avoid or Reduce

Fruits: Most fruits that are sour are to be avoided. These include sour apricots and apples, bananas, sour berries and cherries, cranberries, grapefruit, green grapes, lemons, limes, mangoes, sour oranges, papayas, peaches, persimmons, unripe pineapples and plums, rhubarb, strawberries, and tamarind.

Vegetables: Avoid vegetables that are pungent, such as garlic, onion, hot peppers, and radishes. Other vegetables that are not recommended include beets, carrots, chard, green chilies, eggplant, horseradish, mustard greens, hot peppers, spinach, sweet potatoes, tomatoes, turnips, watercress, and seaweeds.

Grains: Minimize brown rice, buckwheat, corn, dry oats, millet, quinoa, and rye.

Beans: Beans are not especially recommended. If you are going to eat beans, you'll want to see that they're not cooked in lard, which will be aggravating. You may want to avoid lentils.

Dairy: Avoid salted butter, buttermilk, hard or salted cheeses, egg yolks, sour cream, and yogurt.

Meat and fish: Avoid beef, dark chicken, duck, egg yolks, salt-water fish and seafood, lamb, pork, and dark turkey.

Nuts and seeds: Most nuts and seeds are not recommended.

Oils: Animal oils are the most heating and are thus the ones you most want to avoid. You may also want to avoid almond, apricot, corn, olive oil, safflower, and sesame oils, as well as margarine.

Herbs and spices: Minimize your intake of pungent spices and herbs, as well as rock salt and salt. You may especially want to avoid cayenne and chili peppers. Watch out for basil, bay leaf, black pepper, celery seed, cloves, fenugreek, garlic, dry ginger, asafetida (also known as hing), horseradish, mustard, nutmeg, oregano, paprika, rosemary, sage, and thyme.

Sweeteners: Avoid honey unless it's fresh, raw, and unprocessed; also avoid white sugar and molasses.

Dietary Guidelines for Kapha

Kaphas don't need to eat as frequently or as much as other types; sometimes fasting is recommended, and in general, it is better to eat smaller portions. Breakfast can often be skipped; the main meal should be at noon; and heavy foods should be avoided, especially at the end of the day. Dry cooking methods like baking, sautéing, and broiling are preferable. Kaphas do well with salads, raw vegetables, and fruits. It is generally best to stay away from alcohol, but some caffeine is all right. A hazard for Kapha types is that they will eat out of emotional need rather than real hunger; it is best to eat only when there is genuine hunger. To counter the cold, heavy, and moist qualities of Kapha, foods should be warm, light, and drying. Tastes to emphasize are bitter, astringent, and pungent.

Foods to Emphasize

Fruits: Fruit is not emphasized, as it increases the Kapha tendency toward excess water; however, some dry fruit is all right. Astringent fruits are the best; sweet fruits are less helpful. Apples, apricots, berries, cherries, cranberries, dry figs, peaches, pears, persimmons, pomegranates, prunes, and raisins are okay.

Vegetables: Because vegetables are generally light and dry, most are appropriate. The ones to emphasize are those with pungent and bitter tastes. Here are some of the vegetables that can be eaten: artichokes, asparagus, beets, broccoli, brussels sprouts, cabbage, carrots, cauliflower, celery, cilantro, eggplant, fennel, garlic, green beans, green chilies, kale, leafy greens, leaks, lettuce, mushrooms, mustard greens, onions, parsley, peas, peppers, potatoes, radishes, spinach, sprouts, cooked tomatoes, turnips, and watercress.

Grains: Many grains are not so helpful because of their heaviness, so they should be eaten in small quantities. Some grains that can be eaten are barley, buckwheat, cereals, corn, millet, muesli, oat bran, dry oats, polenta, rye, sago, sprouted wheat, tapioca, and wheat bran.

Beans: Because beans are drying and increase air, they help to pacify excess Kapha, with the exception of kidney beans and soybeans. Adzuki beans, black beans, black-eyed peas, red and brown lentils, lima beans, navy beans, dried peas, pinto beans, split peas, and white beans are okay.

Dairy: Dairy tends to contribute to Kapha aggravation by creating excess mucus and congestion. Some products that can be eaten are buttermilk, goat's milk, and goat's cheese.

Meat and fish: Meat tends to increase Kapha. Those that are more acceptable are white chicken and turkey, eggs, and freshwater fish.

Nuts and seeds: Most nuts and seeds are not good for Kapha, though they are better as a protein source than meat or dairy. Sunflower and pumpkin seeds may be all right in small quantities.

Oils: Oils should be used very lightly, as they increase the Kapha qualities of heaviness and moisture. Animal oils like lard are the worst; good vegetable oils to use are corn, mustard, and sunflower.

Herbs and spices: All spices are good for Kapha, with the exception of salt, which can lead to excess water retention.

Sweeteners: Honey and fruit juice concentrates are the only sweeteners that are recommended.

Foods to Avoid or Reduce

Fruits: Most sweet and sour fruits are to be avoided because they can increase water and mucus in the body. These include bananas, coconut, dates, fresh figs, grapefruit, kiwi, melons, oranges, papaya, pineapple, plums, rhubarb, tamarind, and watermelon.

Vegetables: Sweet and juicy vegetables are not recommended. These include corn, cucumber, olives, sweet potatoes, pumpkin, winter squash, raw tomatoes, and zucchini.

Grains: Because of the heavy nature of grains, they are not particularly recommended for Kapha types. Grains to minimize are brown and white rices, oats, and wheat. Breads that have yeast tend to be mucus-forming and should also be avoided.

Beans: Avoid kidney beans and soybeans, as well as soy products like soy cheese, soy flour, soy powder, soy sauce, tofu, and miso.

Dairy: Dairy products should be kept to a minimum. Avoid salted butter, cheese, cottage cheese, cream, ice cream, milk, sour cream, and yogurt.

Meat and fish: Avoid beef, lamb, pork, and seafood (shrimp may be all right).

Nuts and seeds: Avoid most nuts and seeds.

Oils: Most oils are not good for Kapha. These include almond, avocado, apricot, coconut, ghee, olive, peanut, safflower, soy, and sesame oils; margarine is also not recommended.

Herbs and spices: The only spice to avoid is salt, as it increases retention of water.

Sweeteners: Honey and fruit juice concentrates are the only sweeteners that are recommended; avoid barley malt, fructose, maple syrup, molasses, rice syrup, turbinado, and white sugar.

Obviously, if you eat out, as many people do in this day and age, you will have far less control over the food that you put into your body. You can, however, still pay close attention to what you're being served and the manner in which it's prepared. In the *Ayurvedic Cookbook,* authors Morningstar and Desai suggest that "food prepared with openness, clarity, cleanliness, and awareness can mitigate a lot of the less positive qualities of the food itself." Make a point to patronize restaurants that feel as though care is given to the preparation of the food. Other than that, you can continue to observe the same principles that you would if you were preparing your own food.

four

GOING DEEPER

Assessing the Other Influences on Your Health

Good health infuses us with a general sense of well-being and aliveness. The body feels strong and supple; our senses are alert; and the mind is clear and open. There's the sense that we have plenty of energy and capacity for whatever life throws in our path, and we have a feeling of moving effortlessly from moment to moment.

Both Ayurveda and yoga describe good health as a state in which the body's prana, or life-force, is flowing smoothly and evenly throughout the body. You can think of prana as a kind of intelligence within the body that flows and communicates between cells. This prana travels through subtle channels called *nadis*. It is said that there are as many as 72,000 of these nadis, though some texts mention more. To create and maintain good health, then, it is essential that we keep the nadis clear so that there can be a healthy flow of prana. It is when prana encounters obstruction that we run into trouble.

When we are in a healthy state, the doshas are fairly balanced. It is normal for there to be imbalances from time to time, but these are *temporary* imbalances: a healthy person manages to reestablish the correct doshic balance in a fairly short period of time.

In Ayurveda, disease is seen as a long process that doesn't just happen overnight, out of the blue. Disease can actually begin when the doshas go out of balance *and are allowed to stay that way for a prolonged period of time.*

As we mentioned in chapter 3, when the doshas are thrown out of balance, the first thing to be affected is agni, the digestive fire, which becomes weakened. This in turn leads to the accumulation of ama, which is a toxic substance that begins to spread into the body and then creates clogging so that prana is no longer able to flow freely.

The nature and severity of disease depend on how long ama has been building up and how far into the body it has penetrated. Diseases that are addressed in their earlier stages are, as you might expect, much easier to deal with than those that have gone on for a long time and have penetrated more deeply. For this reason, Ayurveda puts a great deal of emphasis on *prevention* of disease. The idea is to become more and more attuned to the small signals of the body and mind that signify changes in the balance of the doshas; then you may be able to make appropriate adjustments to rebalance the doshas, and the chances of avoiding disease and enjoying good health will be much greater.

Many things can contribute to the imbalance of the doshas: wrong diet, stress, repressed or negative emotions, and unhelpful habits and lifestyles. The seasons, as well as our age, can influence doshic balance. Some of these influences can be controlled, while some are completely out of our control. If we at least understand what a few of these influences are, we'll be able to make better choices and take steps—where we can—to safeguard our health. Below are some of the main contributors to doshic imbalance.

Diet. Good diet is fundamental to good health. If you are eating poor-quality food, you will definitely be building up ama—toxins—in your system. Likewise, if your diet is not appropriate for your type and your digestion is not strong, you will, in effect, be constantly straining your system to cope with what you put into it, and that, too, can cause ama and could eventually lead to disease. Chapter 3 covers diet in some detail, so if you haven't read it, you may wish to do so now.

Stress. More and more people seem to be suffering from stress. Stress is now being implicated as a major contributing factor to the development of all kinds of life-threatening conditions like high blood pressure, heart disease, and ulcers. Stress is quite possibly linked with allergies as well as strange and mysterious illnesses, like chronic fatigue syndrome, that are on the rise, particularly in large cities.

To some degree, stress is something that we can avoid if we make different choices about how we spend our time. Many stresses, however, are beyond our control, like when someone we love dies or when we are laid off from a job.

The doshas are very sensitive to stress and can easily be set out of balance by it. During especially stressful times, we may want to be watchful for indications of doshic imbalance in the form of negative emotions like fear and anxiety (a sign of aggravated Vata) or anger and aggression (Pitta aggravation) or lethargy and depression (Kapha aggravation). Then, even if we can't change the actual circumstances that upset us, we can at least do other things to support ourselves in coping. Ayurveda offers many simple and helpful tools for dealing with stress, like breathing practices (pranayama), yoga, meditation, self-massage, and others for creating a more balanced state. These practices are described in some detail in chapters 5 and 6.

Habits and lifestyle. We can unwittingly create imbalance in the doshas through some of our habits and lifestyle choices.

Take Tanya, for example, who is a Vata type and works several nights a week in a loud and busy restaurant. Her schedule is somewhat erratic, and many times she is called in at the last minute to do someone else's shift. The work is intense and requires a lot of energy. She comes home late at night and is often exhausted.

Such a work situation is not at all suitable for a Vata person like Tanya. The hours are irregular, and one of the things Vatas most need is regularity. Also, Vatas need to have adequate rest, and staying up late at night is not so good for them. The loud restaurant environment is too stimulating for a sound-sensitive Vata person. And, because Vatas tend to have less stamina, restaurant work may be too physically challenging. Even though Tanya is very health conscious and takes care of herself in other ways, she is continually throwing her doshas out of balance by continuing the work that she does.

Tanya's situation is more extreme because her work takes up a lot of her time and is therefore a big part of her life. But many of us do plenty of smaller things on a regular basis that can also be unbalancing for us.

Because the doshas are influenced by our senses, even the simple act of listening to music that is too loud or watching a violent movie can disturb their balance. Neglecting to exercise or doing the wrong kind of exercise or doing exercise in the wrong way can upset doshic balance. Our doshas are also sensitive to our emotional life, so when we get lost in negative emotional reactions, our doshas are negatively affected as well.

Again, some things are beyond our control. However, the *awareness* of how easily our doshas can be aggravated can help us be more mindful and take better care of ourselves when possible. Even the smaller daily choices that we make can affect us, so, knowing this, you may be motivated to begin choosing differently. Perhaps, the next time you get into your car, instead of automatically turning on the radio, you'll take a few moments just to quietly reflect. Or maybe you'll consider skipping the more violent TV program in favor of one that is more peaceful and calm.

Weather and seasons. As we mentioned in chapter 3, seasonal changes affect the doshas. From March through May, the Kapha dosha increases, making you more vulnerable to Kapha problems, such as congestion, allergies, and hay fever. From June through September, Pitta tends to increase, and with it the chances that you will have Pitta aggravation, like heartburn, stomach acidity, and insomnia. From October through February, Vata can rise, and you may be more prone to Vata problems, such as headaches, constipation, and arthritis. Be aware that these seasonal shifts are powerful and can influence you!

Obviously, you can't change the weather, but you can take steps to protect yourself from the weather. If you know that early spring is flu season due to increased Kapha, you can make a point of wearing warmer clothes or take teas that will bolster your immune system. To avoid Pitta problems in the summer, you can arrange your schedule so that you do your exercise in the early morning or evening rather than in the middle of the day.

During the fall, when Vata increases and can result in increased dryness, you may want to make sure your skin is getting ample moisturizing. Even better, you may want to spend more time doing self-massage, one of the Ayurvedic techniques that is discussed later on. Many of these suggested measures are intuitive, but it helps to think more consciously about why you are taking them. In chapter 7, you'll find more detailed suggestions for how to make seasonal adjustments to your daily routine.

Age. In Ayurveda, different doshas dominate different ages. Kapha is the dosha that is responsible for the creation and strength of all structures, so even before we are born, while we are still in the womb, we are in a Kapha stage. This rapid and intensive period of growth and development continues through childhood. During these early years, children have more of a Kapha tendency toward plumpness and softness; they are also more prone to Kapha problems like mucus production, congestion, and colds.

As they grow older and move into adulthood, they progress into a Pitta-dominated stage. This is when a great deal of intellectual development can occur, which is one of the areas that the Pitta dosha controls. Also, there is more drive and ambition (characteristic of Pittas), and life is usually much busier at this time of life. Young adults are more liable to get Pitta disorders like acne; in later years there may be more of a tendency toward Pitta problems like ulcers and stomach acidity.

Finally, as we move into old age, we begin a more Vata-dominated stage of life. Older people often shrink in size, becoming lighter than they once were, and they can develop dryness, leading to Vata problems like constipation and dry skin. Memory can become less clear, also a characteristic of Vata imbalance.

It's useful to bear these stages in mind as we make certain choices. If you have a young child, for instance, you might want to give your child foods that are more drying, to counteract the phlegm that tends to build up during this time, or use Ayurvedic herbs to help bolster your child's immune system.

If you are in the midst of the busy Pitta stage of life, there may be more need in your routine for cooling and calming practices, like meditation and relaxation. Or, if you are an elderly person, you might want to be on the lookout for Vata dryness and take measures to keep this from getting out of hand by avoiding drying foods and eating more moistening ones.

THE DIFFERENT STAGES OF DISEASE

If you are able to keep your doshas in balance most of the time, then your health will likely be good. If not, then you may be setting yourself up for trouble later on.

Ayurveda sees disease as a process that is initiated by doshic imbalance, and this occurs long before the disease itself actually manifests. This early stage is known as the *accumulation* phase. Here, the doshas begin to build up in their "home" sites—those areas of the body in which they normally reside. So Vata accumulates in the colon; Pitta gathers in the intestines; and Kapha builds up in the stomach. At this stage, it is relatively easy to restore balance through proper diet, exercise, relaxation, and many of the other Ayurvedic techniques that will be discussed later.

If the doshas are not restored to their proper balance but instead are allowed to continue accumulating, then the next phase of disease begins: this is the *aggravated* or *disturbed* phase, in which the home sites of the doshas become so overloaded that the doshas begin leaking into other parts of the body. At this stage it is still possible to restore balance through applying the appropriate corrective measures.

After the disturbed stage comes the more serious *spreading* or *flooding* phase, in which the doshas seep into the blood, moving more definitively into other sites of the body. To restore the balance of the doshas now requires more extreme measures in the form of a cleansing program, known as *panchakarma*. For this, a person needs the guidance of an Ayurvedic practitioner.

If the doshas are allowed to continue to spread, then they move into areas of the body where there is already some sort of inherent weakness or vulnerability. This phase is known as the *movement* or *deposition* phase. Vasant Lad explains in *The Complete Book of Ayurvedic Home Remedies* that this newly arrived dosha "creates confusion within the cellular intelligence of the weaker tissue and overwhelms it, changing its normal qualities and functions." He goes on to say that "the quality of the aggravated dosha suppresses the normal qualities of the tissue and combines with it, creating an altered state, changed in structure and function. In this way the 'seeds' of disease begin to sprout."

Manifestation is the next phase. This is when symptoms become obvious, and the person actually gets sick. Following this phase is the *chronic disease* phase, in which the person becomes seriously ill.

Hopefully, as you read this book, you are in good health. Even if you feel relatively well, you'll be able to benefit more fully from Ayurveda's home practices with a little guidance. If you do have difficulties with your health, you will definitely want to seek out an Ayurvedic practitioner to help you structure an appropriate Ayurvedic course of treatment. It's worth mentioning here that Ayurveda does address very serious illnesses and conditions. In fact, often people turn to Ayurveda when they feel they have run out of other options. For such problems, it's important to find a reputable and skilled practitioner.

Finding an Ayurvedic practitioner is not unlike finding any good health practitioner. One of the best ways is through word of mouth. Ask around: if you have friends or colleagues who consult an Ayurvedic practitioner, you can ask them what their experience has been and how they feel about their practitioner.

If you are taking yoga classes, you may want to ask your yoga teacher for recommendations. Many yoga teachers are not yet familiar with Ayurveda, but some of them are, so it doesn't hurt to try. Particularly if you live in an urban area, there may be an Ayurvedic center of some kind: you can always look in the phone book or on the Internet. Also, if there's an Indian population where you live, you may find Indian-product stores that also have bulletin boards where resources are listed. Many of the available Ayurveda books also have a list of resources, so you can always check those. (At the back of this book is a list of book sources that you can consult.)

Once you get the name of someone, you'll want to have some idea of what that person's background is. Many people who have become skilled in Ayurveda have spent time in institutions in India or have studied privately with an Indian doctor of Ayurveda. With the increasing interest in Ayurveda in the West, there are many more graduates from Western schools as well.

You'll want to know that the person you choose is first and foremost a healer and is not motivated by commercial or financial interests: this is the sign of someone who is working in the true spirit of Ayurveda. Many practitioners in the West have set fees for their services, but if you have the need, you can always ask if there is a sliding scale available.

Bear in mind that if you are working with an Indian (who was actually born and raised in India), you may encounter some cultural differences. You may find, for instance, that an Indian practitioner might seem a bit austere in manner. This does not necessarily indicate a lack of compassion or caring but is often simply a difference in style.

Ultimately, the main thing is to feel comfortable enough with your practitioner to trust and follow his or her suggestions. Let your intuition be your guide. Once you have decided, you will get the best results if you are respectful and come with a genuine curiosity, interest, and openness.

WHAT TO EXPECT FROM AN AYURVEDIC CONSULTATION

An Ayurvedic practitioner will want to find out what your type is and what the current state of balance or imbalance in the doshas is. If you are having a particular problem, it will be important to try to identify the underlying cause. Is the problem in your diet? Something in your lifestyle or habits? Does it have to do with your age, your constitution, or the weather? It will be important to understand more about the nature of your problem: what its exact symptoms are, how long it's been going on, and how serious it is.

To assess your state of health, different diagnostic techniques will be used. A skilled and experienced practitioner of Ayurveda is able to tell a great deal about you just from listening to your pulses, but typically, other diagnostic tools are used as well. Different parts of the body will be examined. For instance, a tongue exam indicates how much ama (toxicity) has built up in your system and also where in your body the ama is likely to be concentrated. Your eyes may be peered into. Parts of your body may be prodded or squeezed to see if there are sore or sensitive areas that could indicate weaknesses in different tissues and organ systems of the body. In addition, you may be asked a lot of questions about your diet, sleep patterns, relationships and emotional life, and general daily habits.

Based on the findings, you will be given a particular regimen to follow, which may involve diet, exercise, pranayama (breathing techniques), and other self-care practices. If you already feel fairly healthy, and your lifestyle is well balanced and health promoting, the program you are given may be less involved. However, it's possible that a skilled practitioner will pick up on the earliest warning signs of an imbalance that you yourself cannot yet feel. This is good, because the sooner you can detect imbalance and correct it, the better. If necessary, some sort of detoxification program will be prescribed, like panchakarma, followed by a program for rebuilding the body's strength and immunity. Part of your treatment may involve taking herbs.

If you are in good health, then you may need only one or two consultations. If you are dealing with a more serious condition, it's possible that you'll need to work with a practitioner for a while. Because of its gentle, noninvasive methods, Ayurveda does not work overnight but may require time as well as dedication and patience on your part.

five

HEALING THE BODY

In Ayurveda, we can maintain health and heal the body through several different means. The correct use of herbs, self-massage, exercise, and yoga will all help restore and maintain doshic balance. If necessary, an Ayurvedic practitioner may also prescribe the cleansing process known as pancha-karma.

When you consult with a practitioner of Ayurveda, you may be in excellent health, and perhaps just a few preventative measures will be prescribed. It is likely, however, that even if you feel well, your practitioner will find signs of some toxicity in your system. If you are in the accumulation or aggravation stages of disease (long before any actual disease manifestation), you will want to be sure to reestablish the balance of your doshas so that you avoid further buildup. This will be relatively easy to do through the right regimen.

Many powerful and healing herbs are available to us through Ayurveda. Most of the herbs that are prescribed today have, in fact, been used therapeutically for thousands of years, and so a great deal is known about their actions on the human body. The system of classification that Ayurveda uses is quite complex and sophisticated, and it is far beyond the scope of this book to go into much detail about this subject; however, if you are interested in this aspect of Ayurveda, books listed in the sources section at the back will give you much more detailed information.

To give you a basic introduction, herbs are derived from plants and can be made from the roots, bark, stems, leaves, seeds, or flowers. There are many different ways to prepare and ingest herbs. They can be used as teas and decoctions. They can be mixed into foods or liquids in their fresh state, ground up, or powdered. Sometimes they are powdered and then put into capsules and taken that way.

Like foods, herbs have different characteristics, and their use can produce different effects. In general, six classifications are used to describe herbs (for some herbs, only five are used). Taste is one classification. Herbs usually have two or more tastes, so an herb might be both bitter and astringent, for example. Another classification is the herb's attributes, or qualities; for

instance, an herb might be described as being both oily and
light. The potency of an herb, which is also its primary effect, is
described as either heating or cooling. Each herb also has a
long-term effect, a general action, and usually a specific action
as well.

You can think of herbs as working in a similar way as foods.
So, in deciding which herbs to use, you'll want to select those
whose characteristics are the *opposite* of the condition that you
are trying to balance. Suppose, for example, that you are experiencing a Kapha imbalance, such as a cold or flu. Kapha is generally cold, heavy, and wet. That means you'd want to use an
herb that has opposite qualities and is warm, light, and dry.
There is another consideration, too: an herb can have a long-
term effect that is not necessarily obvious from its initial taste.
For example, pippli, which is an Indian pepper, has a pungent
taste, but its long-term effect is sweet.

This may seem confusing because it is! Keep in mind when
using herbs that you don't have to try to figure it out all by
yourself. In fact, you shouldn't. Plenty of resources exist that
will tell you specifically what the herb is good for and how to
use it. Also, should you choose to work with an Ayurvedic practitioner, you will be given detailed instructions about herbal
dosages and use. Over time, as you work with different herbs,
you may find that you gradually become more sensitized to
their effects.

As mentioned earlier, Ayurveda employs massage as one of its healing techniques. There is a complex system of points called *marma* points, which are similar to the points used in acupressure and acupuncture. These points are connected to one another by the nadis, which conduct our life-force, or prana, throughout the body. By working particular marmas, we stimulate the flow of prana in those areas of the body. If you want to experience an Ayurvedic massage, you can usually find someone through the same sources that you would use to find an Ayurvedic practitioner. Not all practitioners offer massage, but they can usually refer you to someone who does.

Though it is quite wonderful to receive a massage from someone else, it can be very nourishing to give this wonderful gift to yourself, too. *Abhyanga,* or self-massage, is one of the delicious tools for healing that is encouraged in an Ayurvedic lifestyle.

Massaging yourself will put you in a more relaxed and calm frame of mind, and it will help you rid yourself of stress. It can also give you a new way to relate to and nourish yourself. There is nothing complicated about self-massage, and anyone can easily learn to do it.

Abhyanga is typically done in the morning, though it is a nice way to finish the day, too. A nighttime massage can help you relax and go to sleep if you tend to have any insomnia problems.

What you'll want is a clean place to massage yourself, some oil, and a couple of towels. Pick an appropriate oil for your particular needs. Sesame oil is commonly used and is especially good for lowering Vata conditions; you may want to use this if you're feeling anxious or fearful. Coconut or sunflower oils are helpful for cooling and calming Pitta aggravation; and Kapha conditions can be aided by using corn oil or mustard oil. Make sure to store your oils in a cool, dry place so that they don't go rancid.

Ideally, you'll want to heat the oil slightly before using it. You can do this by putting four or five tablespoons of oil in a pan and briefly heating the pan on the stove. Another way is to run some hot water over your oil bottle for a few minutes, or let the oil bottle stand for a minute or two in a container of hot water. Make sure that you don't overheat the oil, and test it before you use it!

Because you will be using oil, the ideal place to do your massage is in the bathroom, where it doesn't matter so much if you spill a little. You may want to cover the floor with a plastic sheet or large garbage bag; then place a towel or two on top of this, and station yourself there.

If you have the time, set aside fifteen minutes or more for your massage. If you're pressed for time, don't deprive yourself: even just a few minutes will make you feel better.

You'll move in a downward direction as you massage yourself. Start by putting some oil in your palm, rub the oil between your palms, and then begin massaging your scalp. The scalp responds nicely to fairly vigorous stroking; this is a great way to wake yourself up in the morning.

Next, proceed to your face, forehead, temples, and neck. You can use a gentle circular motion, without pressing too hard. From there, move to your shoulders and upper back. Then proceed down your arms, paying more attention to your joints as you go along and using a circular motion over the wrists, elbows, and shoulders.

As you need to, replenish your oil. You can massage the chest, abdomen, and lower back, again using mostly circular strokes. Long, strong strokes are good for the legs, though you may want to use circular motions once more over the hip, knee, and ankle joints.

Finally, massage the feet. Do not neglect the soles of the feet, as they have many important marma points that correspond to the body's vital organs. You'll also want to get in between and around the toes.

When you're done, if it's possible, leave the oil on for a while: that way it can soak into the skin and you will absorb more of the balancing and nourishing properties of the oils. Traditionally, flour is used to rub the oil off the body, but this is not very practical, so you may just want to wash the oil off in the shower.

It's recommended that you massage yourself every morning. You may want to try this for a week and see how it feels. You will likely find it a greatly nourishing practice that you won't want to stop!

Everyone needs exercise to stay healthy. When we exercise regularly, we become stronger, more flexible, and more coordinated. Our stamina improves, circulation becomes more efficient, and our immune systems are bolstered. Exercise helps us keep our digestion functioning smoothly, and we are able to more effectively rid the body of toxins; it also helps us regulate our appetite and weight. When we're in a regular pattern of exercise, we sleep better, think better, and generally feel better.

It's clear, then, that when we don't exercise, we're not supporting our health. In fact, inadequate exercise can be detrimental, and the chances are much greater of eventually developing serious diseases like diabetes, colon cancer, and osteoporosis. For Americans in particular, the risk of developing heart disease is very high.

On the other hand, getting too much exercise, or the wrong kind of exercise for your type, can also be damaging. When you exercise in a way that takes you too far beyond your natural capacity, and especially if you do this consistently, you end up straining your body and creating more work for the body to do in order to recover.

In Ayurveda it's suggested that you exercise in a way that works you but doesn't strain you. You need to find the right kind of exercise—something that feels challenging and that *you also enjoy*—and then make sure that you are doing that activity in a way that benefits you optimally. An excellent book that discusses exercise in depth and from an Ayurvedic perspective is *Body, Mind, and Sport* by John Douillard.

Just as you choose foods that are appropriate for your type, you will also want to select exercise based on your type. Kaphas have the sturdiest constitutions and generally have the greatest capacity for intense, sustained physical activity. Vatas are at the other end of the spectrum: their energy tends to come in fits and starts, and they can easily deplete themselves with too much physical activity. Pittas fall somewhere in the middle: they have an average capacity for physical exertion. Because you may well be a combination of two different types, you'll want to keep in mind which of the two types is dominant, and you can also factor in things like your age, any current imbalances in the doshas, the weather, and so forth.

Vatas and Exercise

Vatas are often light, flexible, and quick moving. Many Vatas are attracted to sports that require fast, agile movement, like running, for example; but actually, what a typical Vata needs is to slow down and do something more calming, grounding, and nurturing.

A gentle, flowing style of yoga practice is excellent for a Vata type; this will be physically challenging but in a calming and soothing way. Some sports that may be appropriate include swimming, golfing, sailing, and bicycling. Walking is also an excellent form of exercise. You'll want to make sure that if you're exercising outside, you have adequate clothing to keep you protected from the elements.

When exercising, it's important to look for signs of straining. If you don't feel well while you're exercising or afterward, that could indicate that you are doing too much or the wrong kind of exercise. Try cutting back a little, or try something else.

Pittas and Exercise

Pittas have a moderate physical capacity. They are generally well proportioned and can be quite athletic. Being by nature very focused and driven to succeed, they are often drawn to competitive sports, but these activities do not necessarily bring out the best in a Pitta type! Pittas need to ease up—on themselves and usually on everyone around them, too. Exercise that will help them relax, cool down, and get into a more meditative frame of mind is the most helpful.

A cooling yoga practice that is adequately challenging may be just what a Pitta type needs. Swimming can be therapeutic, as water helps to cool the fiery nature of Pitta. A few other sports that a Pitta may enjoy are sailing, skiing, golfing, and bicycling. Also, though it may not be so appealing to a Pitta type, walking can be very therapeutic.

Because Pittas tend to run hot, you'll want to be on the lookout for signs of overheating, especially when the weather is warmer; if you do get overheated, you may find that you feel depleted later on. Also, if you find your temper flaring during your exercise, you may want to try some other form of exercise.

Kaphas and Exercise

Kaphas have the greatest capacity for physical exercise and also the greatest need for it. This is sometimes difficult for them, as they can have a tendency to laze around and avoid physical challenges.

Because of their reluctance to physically exert themselves, Kaphas can sometimes suffer sluggish digestion and depression. Strong exercise like running, rowing, or martial arts, for example, can help counter those imbalances. Walking is also good for Kaphas, but they should walk at a fast clip. An intense, athletic yoga practice that induces sweating is a great form of exercise for a Kapha type.

Like Vata types, Kaphas should be careful not to get cold if exercising outdoors. It's also important for a Kapha to keep at it and not give in to those sedentary tendencies. However, you don't want to take this to any extreme, and just like anyone, you'll want to avoid overdoing it. This is especially true if you have fallen into the Kapha tendency to be overweight and are just beginning to exercise; you'll want to begin slowly and build up gradually and sensibly.

Eight steps, or limbs, as they are known, make up the study and practice of classical yoga. The third limb of yoga, *asana* practice, involves postures and movements. This is the aspect of yoga that is most familiar to Westerners. Several different styles of yoga are typically found in the West, and certain ones are more suited to Vata, Pitta, and Kapha types.

There are hundreds, perhaps thousands, of different postures, and each posture can have particular effects on the body and mind. The way in which a posture is held can also affect how it works on the practitioner. In typical public yoga classes, students are instructed do the same postures in the same order and the same way. A skilled teacher, of course, can provide modifications and alternatives for a student who has special conditions, but this obviously cannot be done for the whole class.

Originally, however, yoga was taught one-on-one so that a student could learn a sequence of postures that were tailored especially for him or her, taking into consideration age, sex, constitution, state of health, and stage of life. This approach makes sense, for what works for one person may not be helpful for another; in fact, what may be beneficial for one kind of person can actually have adverse effects on another.

In considering beginning a yoga practice, it's helpful to know a bit about some of the forms of yoga that are available, as they can vary quite a bit, and one form or another may be more suitable, depending on your type.

Ashtanga Yoga

One of the most popular styles offered in the West today is Ashtanga yoga. This offers an athletic, high-powered practice. The postures are done in a set sequence that you will become familiar with after you've attended a class a few times. There is a lot of emphasis on breathing, using a steady, audible breath that passes through the nose. The heat is turned up high and the windows are kept closed so that your body is forced to sweat.

The person who can probably benefit the most from this style is the Kapha person: Ashtanga will definitely get you moving! The strongly athletic quality of this style increases circulation and pumps up the metabolism, countering the slower-moving system of typical Kaphas. Because it's almost impossible to avoid sweating profusely, Ashtanga yoga can be very cleansing, removing many toxins from the body and thus decreasing the tendency toward stagnation so common in Kapha types. Also, Kaphas may find the heat itself appealing because they tend to dislike cool conditions. The intense physicality of the practice is no problem for Kapha people because, once they get going, they usually have the greatest endurance and strength of all the different types.

Because many Pitta types have an innate energy and drive, they may feel tempted to take on the challenge of an Ashtanga yoga practice. For a Pitta constitution, however, Ashtanga may not be the right choice at all and may actually aggravate a Pitta imbalance. The somewhat competitive quality of a traditional Ashtanga class can feed into this same quality in Pitta types, and ultimately, the intense heat is fatiguing and drains a Pitta's energy. Some Pittas run so hot that the heat of Ashtanga yoga may make this style less attractive to begin with. Likewise, Vata types would probably fare better with another style of yoga: Ashtanga requires more strength and endurance than typical Vatas have.

Iyengar Yoga

Iyengar yoga is another style of yoga that is now popular in the West. With its attention to the form and details of the postures as well as its slower pace, it is a style that may be more compatible with Pitta and Vata types. Vata people have too much movement in their lives; they can get scattered in too many different directions, so the slow precision of Iyengar yoga practice can give them something to ground themselves with and focus their attention on. Practiced in the right way, Iyengar yoga can help a weaker Vata person build more stamina and strength. This same quality of precision can be appealing to Pitta types, too, who tend to appreciate detail and order. Also, Iyengar yoga can be quite vigorous, and Pittas need a good challenge.

Kundalini Yoga

Kundalini yoga is another form that is becoming more and more popular. This style tends to work with the breath a great deal, and practice often involves repetitive movements leading in and out of the postures, which are done in coordination with the breath.

Kundalini yoga can be quite a vigorous practice, requiring a certain amount of strength. There can sometimes be an atmosphere of pushing oneself and keeping up no matter what, which may not be beneficial for competitive Pitta types. Also, as a practice, Kundalini yoga may be a little more strenuous than what Vatas need. This style will definitely stir things up, so it may be an especially good form for Kaphas.

Vini Yoga

Vini yoga is similar to Kundalini in that it combines movement with breath. However, it tends to be much softer and gentler; for this reason, it may not be that well suited to Kapha people. Though it may be less appealing to Pitta types, it is actually a very appropriate form, as it is challenging enough without being overly intense. Vatas will find this an attractive style because of the gentle movement; also, the emphasis on breathing will be strengthening to Vatas.

As you read through these descriptions, remember that they are generalizations: it is hard to speak about a particular style of yoga being entirely one way or another, as much of your experience rests on the teacher, and teachers can vary quite a bit. Ultimately, you just need to go out and try some classes, find a teacher that you really like, and see what works best for you.

PRACTICING YOGA

It is beyond the scope of this book to go into yoga postures in any depth, but it may be helpful to know a few things about how these postures can be used to benefit you. It will also be useful to think about what attitude you should try to cultivate as you're practicing yoga.

Vatas and Yoga

Vatas can be a little flighty and rushed, and it's important to drop that habit the moment you begin your yoga practice. This is a time to slow down and really pay attention to the experience that is happening right now. If you don't come to your yoga practice with this intention, you may rush into postures too quickly and, as a result, get hurt.

It is particularly good for a Vata person to try to do yoga on a regular basis, preferably daily, and at the same time of day (mornings are the best time). This may be in opposition to your habit of avoiding routine, but after a while, you may discover that the ritual of yoga practice can be very grounding and calming.

The kinds of postures that will be helpful to you are ones that promote flexibility in the spine and in many of the joints of the body. This is because Vatas can tend to have dry, cracking joints, and unless you work to change that tendency, it may get quite a bit worse as you get older.

You'll also want to work on strengthening postures, practicing them regularly and gradually building up your stamina. It will feel good to grow stronger, and this will make you more steady, both physically and mentally.

Because the Vata dosha's primary site is in the colon, you'll find postures that work primarily with the pelvic cavity particularly beneficial. Postures in which the knees are drawn up toward the chest or twisting postures may be especially useful for relieving gas—one of the common discomforts that Vatas suffer.

Finally, *shavasana,* or relaxation, is a necessary practice for Vatas. It comes at the end of yoga practice and lasts for about ten minutes or more. It involves simply lying on the floor without moving and then consciously relaxing every residual bit of tension in the body and mind. Often Vatas are ready to leap up and go on to the next thing, so shavasana can be particularly challenging. If you can just stick with it for a while, you will discover that this part of your practice is the soothing reward for your earlier efforts. This step is actually very important: it is what the whole of your yoga practice builds up to. Shavasana is meant to prepare you for the next step in yoga practice, which is pranayama (breathing exercises); from there, you eventually go into deeper meditative practices.

Pittas and Yoga

One of the main challenges for Pittas is to learn to relax and enjoy life rather than trying to control and direct things. Because Pittas can be so attached to competing and achieving, it is helpful for them to choose a style of yoga that will emphasize surrender and relaxation. In general, this is a quality that Pittas may need to bring out in themselves as they practice: instead of striving to do the perfect yoga posture, they will benefit much more from simply relaxing into the pose and allowing it to unfold more organically.

Pittas generally run hot, so postures that are more cooling are best. If you are a Pitta, you may want to deemphasize postures that will make you more "hotheaded," like headstands and backbends (unless you know the proper cooling-down counter poses). The Pitta dosha tends to collect in the region of the solar plexus, so postures like forward bends and seated twists that work this area will be especially beneficial.

Shavasana is a must for a Pitta person. This provides a time to really rest the eyes, which can be overused and strained by the typical Pitta person. Shavasana also presents an opportunity to direct all of the abundant mental energy that Pittas have toward cultivating more inner awareness. This in turn helps prepare the body and mind for deeper meditation.

Kaphas and Yoga

If you are a Kapha, you will want to avoid seated postures and focus more on poses that are stimulating, energizing, and warming. Repetitions of faster-paced sun salutations are recommended; if you break into a sweat, so much the better, as it will help to flush toxins that may be collecting in your body.

Because excess Kapha collects first in the chest cavity, poses that open and stretch the chest will be particularly useful; these will promote more circulation in the chest and can help relieve congestion, coughs, and other Kapha symptoms.

You should do shavasana just as Vata and Pitta types do, but the hazard for you may be falling asleep. Try to relax deeply without going into the unconscious state of sleep. This may be difficult at first, but you will find that with practice it becomes easier.

PANCHAKARMA

When more extreme measures are called for, panchakarma can be a most effective cleansing and detoxifying technique. *Panchakarma* translates as "five actions." It is a five-step therapeutic method that can involve vomiting; purgation or laxative therapy; medicated enema therapy; the administration of medications through the nose; and purification of the blood.

The idea is that through these five actions, the ama, or toxins, will be driven back into the gastrointestinal tract and, from there, out of the body. Panchakarma is a fairly strong and active treatment and should not be used by the weak, sick, or elderly; for such people, a gentler, more passive approach is used instead. Panchakarma should also not be done by pregnant women. In addition, it's important that panchakarma be done under the supervision of someone who is well trained and experienced. This ensures that you will be correctly evaluated, the program will be appropriately tailored for your needs, and you will be skillfully guided through the process. The process is a delicate one, and if it is mistimed, or if you are given the wrong therapy, then you could aggravate the doshas instead of pacifying them.

For it to be effective, panchakarma requires a few weeks, or even a month. Ideally, it is done in an Ayurvedic clinic of some kind, where you can actually stay for the duration of your treatment. (A milder version of panchakarma can also be done at home, and some books include directions for home treatment.) The setting should be clean, attractive, and restful, so that you can relax deeply and focus all your attention on the process as it is unfolding. Wherever you do panchakarma, it's important to try to remove yourself from the usual daily demands and stresses of your life, because the process can be quite powerful, and in addition to making you feel very tired at times, it can bring up a range of emotions.

To begin panchakarma, you first need to make the body ready for its release of toxins, and then the actual purification techniques begin. During this preparatory stage, you will be instructed to drink, on a daily basis, a small amount of ghee (clarified butter). (In the event that you have certain health problems like high cholesterol, blood sugar, or triglycerides, Vasant Lad suggests using flaxseed oil instead.) This preparatory stage can go on for several days. The intention is for the ghee to lubricate the channels of the body, making it easier for ama to travel through them as it makes its way to the gastrointestinal tract and eventually out of the body.

Having completed this stage, you then receive oil massage and take steam baths. During your massages, special upward strokes are used to help encourage the ama to move back into the gastrointestinal tract; the sweating that you do helps to dislodge the toxins from the places in which they are stuck.

After several days of these treatments, which can have a tranquilizing effect on your whole being, and when you are deemed ready, the actual cleansing processes can begin. Each of these special therapies, which you will find briefly described below, is designed to be used only under specific conditions, and there are many conditions for which certain therapies are contraindicated and would therefore not be used at all.

Vamana. The first of the main panchakarma therapies is therapeutic vomiting. The idea is for the body to release wastes through its upper pathways. It is mostly used for balancing Pitta and Kapha excesses, not those of a Vata nature.

Virechana. The second treatment is laxative therapy and involves elimination of wastes through the lower body's pathways. This therapy is used for many Pitta excesses as well as some Kapha excesses.

Basti. Basti consists of a series of enemas that are made out of various herbs and oils. They are meant to help cleanse and purify the colon, which is the primary site of Vata. The Vata dosha is believed to be responsible for the majority of diseases, and it is said that many of these Vata-related diseases can be eliminated through the correct use of this therapy.

Nasya. Nasya involves the insertion of herbs and oils into the nasal passages. It is especially helpful for Vata and Kapha problems but can also aid in Pitta-related problems. In particular, nasya is good for clearing excesses in the sinuses, throat, and head. As you might expect, it can help clear the nasal passages, making breathing easier.

Rakta moksha. Rakta moksha, which involves cleansing the blood, is used much less than it once was. Traditionally, it was performed through bloodletting, which is now illegal in both the United States and Europe. When used correctly, many Pitta problems having to do with skin conditions can be cleared through this therapy.

REBUILDING YOUR BODY

After going through panchakarma, you may feel tired and depleted, especially if your body has had to release a big load of toxins. It is important to spend some time building the body's strength back up.

In addition to giving yourself plenty of time to rest, you'll want to make sure that you observe a diet that is appropriate for your type. It is also recommended that you take certain herbs to help strengthen and rejuvenate you: these are known as *rasayanas*. You'll want to ease back into your regular routine gradually, if possible incorporating some of the other healing therapies that Ayurveda offers, like self-massage, exercise, yoga, pranayama, and meditation.

six

HEALING THE MIND AND SPIRIT

Ayurveda offers many tools for healing and restoring the body. When we use these techniques to benefit our physical health, we are in a better position to begin addressing our mental and spiritual states. This is, in fact, the higher aim of Ayurveda: not just to give us abundant physical health, but also to support our spiritual unfolding. Several practices are available to help us along this path. Shavasana, or relaxation, pranayama practices (breathing exercises), mantra (chanting), and meditation can all have a profound impact on our mental states. Adjunct therapies like color therapy, mineral and metal therapy, gem therapy, and aromatherapy can also be used.

The purpose of both Ayurveda and yoga is to help us become fully realized beings. You can think of this in different ways, according to your beliefs. If you have a belief in God, then you can think of Self-realization as God-realization. If you don't believe in God, you may find it useful to think in terms of becoming all that it is possible to be or reaching your highest potential. The main idea is to get past your normal and limited sense of who you are and realize your true, essential nature, which is already perfect.

What gets in the way of this is a fundamental confusion about who, or what, we are. We think, "I am this body that I see and feel and know so intimately." Or we identify with the roles that we play as a mother or husband or as a person who works in a particular industry. In other words, we tend to think of ourselves as our bodies, our thoughts, and our activities and to think that that is *all* that we are. Much of our culture and modern lifestyle feeds this belief; we're kept in a state of constant stimulation, and it's not so surprising that we have little internal space for any other sense of ourselves. What is needed is to let our senses take a rest so that we can begin to feel what it is like to just be ourselves, without all the unnatural sensory overload that most of us are subjected to on a daily basis.

Many specific techniques are used in an Ayurvedic lifestyle to help our senses relax and allow us to skillfully direct our attention inward. As you become more familiar and comfortable with these techniques, you'll begin to have more of a direct experience of the peace that comes with a still and quiet mind. That in turn may start to open you up to a new experience of yourself, and you may begin to know yourself as something more, or different, than what you had previously perceived. All of this may sound very abstract to you at this point, and it *is* abstract, until you've experienced it. After you've read about all of these methods, begin experimenting for yourself.

Shavasana is a process of actively letting go of the tensions in the body and mind—and then watching carefully to see what arises in your experience as you do that.

Whether or not you practice yoga, relaxation is something that you can incorporate into your life and that will definitely benefit you. You will find that as you learn to consciously relax, some of the sedating behaviors that may have crept into your life—using food, drugs, or alcohol to calm yourself—will begin to drop away.

You will also discover yourself meeting with the mystery of your own existence, for as you rest in relaxation the thought may occur to you that you are still alive, and yet you are doing absolutely nothing! You'll begin to realize that something else other than your own will is sustaining you. This can be a real awakening: you'll start to have glimpses, direct experiences, of a source, your Self—or whatever you wish to call it—that is both in you and in everyone and everything that exists.

Bear in mind that as you bring relaxation into your routine, you may find it challenging. This is common, as most of us are so used to constantly striving, achieving, and producing, that to stop all that activity—even if it's just for a few minutes—can seem contrary to what we've been taught to value. It's important, then, to be patient with yourself as you bring this practice into your life, and also to try to find a method of relaxing that suits your personality type. You may also find that relaxation is easier to do *after* you have physically exerted yourself, either through yoga practice or through some other form of exercise.

Practicing Shavasana

To practice shavasana, find a clean, comfortable place on the floor and stretch yourself out on your back, with your legs slightly apart and your arms resting alongside the body, palms turned upward. Particularly if you have been exerting yourself physically, you may want to cover yourself with a blanket or an extra layer of clothing so that you don't cool off too rapidly. If you find that your back needs a little extra support, you can roll up a blanket or pillow and place it beneath your knees, allowing your legs to fully relax downward. An alternative to this is to plant your feet on the floor, turning them slightly in so that you are a little pigeon-toed, and let your knees rest against each other.

Once you have found a comfortable position, focus on the feeling of your body's weight dropping and relaxing into the floor. Let your awareness travel from the feet all the way up to the head, and be on the lookout for areas of tension. You may notice that even though you thought you were completely relaxed, there is still a little knot of holding in your shoulder blade or in your belly or somewhere else, for that matter. As you take note of these areas of holding, see if you can softly breathe into them: imagine that your breath travels to these places and creates a little more space for the muscles to relax into.

As you proceed, you may also notice that the mind latches onto some thought or other. Just as you let go of tensions in the body, you also want to use shavasana to let go of tensions in the mind. So when you become aware of grabbing onto a thought, give yourself the suggestion to gently relinquish the thought— just for these few minutes—and turn your attention back to your body and the sensations arising in your body as you become more and more restful. One of the most effective ways of turning the mind back to what's happening in the moment is to simply focus your attention on the movement of the breath as it passes in and out of the body. Don't try to control the breath, but just see if you can observe it, allowing it to move through the body freely.

Shavasana is meant to be a *conscious* letting-go of tension, so you want to try to do this practice without falling asleep. (Particularly if you are a Kapha type, you may have this tendency.) Bear in mind that in the beginning, this may be difficult, and you may find yourself nodding off. If you keep trying to do this practice on a regular basis, preferably daily, you'll find that over time it gets easier to relax without falling asleep.

Variations on Shavasana

For some people, slightly different techniques may be more effective to facilitate a relaxed state.

• If you are more of a restless Vata type, you may find it challenging to lie still, even if it's just for a few minutes. What may make the practice a little more accessible is if you intentionally create tension in the body first and then relax. You can do this by simply tightening up the whole body as much as you are able, including the muscles in the face, and holding that tense position for several seconds. As you're tensing the whole body, you can also hold the breath. Then let everything completely relax. Do that a few times. You will definitely find that the body softens more readily after a few repetitions of tensing and then releasing.

• Another approach is to progressively tighten and release individual muscle groups. Start at the toes, and consciously tighten up the toes. Hold the tension in the toes for a few seconds and then release, feeling the toes softening as you let the tension go. Then engage the muscles of the feet by pointing the toes away from you. Again, hold this tension for a few seconds, and then release it. Try flexing the feet so that you feel the musculature of the calves working. Hold for a few seconds, and then let the tension go. Keep moving up the body in this way, until you've reached the crown of your head. By then, you will feel much more relaxed than when you started out.

• For people who are visually oriented, as Pitta types often are, it can be helpful to use a technique that uses your visual imagination. Some people like to envision a light that passes through the body—either moving from the feet to the crown of the head, or vice versa—and as the light travels through the body, it creates a feeling of space and ease. Keep circulating the light up and down the body, feeling any residual tension draining away with each pass of the light. After a while, you may find that you can just sense a light permeating the whole body.

• You may also want to experiment with imagining a total *absence* of light. For this it will be useful to have an eye pillow that you rest over your eyes to block out the light. If you don't have an eye pillow, you can use a dark towel over the eyes instead. Make sure that the light is completely blocked. Then imagine the darkness engulfing the eyes. From there, allow the darkness to seep down through the eyes into the brain. Then let the darkness travel down through the body until the whole body feels as though it is black. From there you can let the blackness move outward into the room and eventually into the space beyond the room, until you have the feeling of being completely absorbed by darkness. This can be a deeply relaxing experience that is especially beneficial to the eyes. Pitta people tend to overuse their eyes, so this technique may be especially relevant for them.

• Some people are not at all visually oriented and respond instead to sound. You may find that the best way for you to relax is to put on a favorite piece of soothing music. Recordings of natural sounds, like birdcalls or ocean waves, can have a quieting effect on the body and mind. If sound provides the way in to a deeper state of relaxation, then by all means use this tool.

All of these techniques aim to do the same thing: to create a feeling of deep ease and relaxation in the body and mind. Try out a few methods, and see which seem to be most effective for you. Then see if you can bring a little conscious relaxation in to your life on a daily basis. In yoga practice, shavasana is a preparation for pranayama, which involves regulating and quieting the fluctuations of the breath. This in turn helps to bring the mind in to a still more quiet place, in preparation for deeper states of meditation.

PRANAYAMA

The term *pranayama* can be broken down into its two parts: *prana,* meaning life-force, and *ayama,* meaning to stretch or extend. So one way to translate pranayama is "to stretch or extend the life-force."

Pranayama involves becoming more mindful of the breath and learning to breathe more consciously. Because breathing is an activity that we do without thinking, most of us have little or no awareness of the way we breathe. If we look more closely at

the breath, though, we can see that how we breathe is intimately linked with our mind states. We've all had direct experiences of this connection: when we are frightened or nervous,
the breath tends to become more shallow, rapid, and irregular.
On the other hand, when we're in a relaxed and balanced state,
the breath is usually deeper, slower, and more even.

Research backs this up: psychological factors like emotional stability, confidence, and calmness are equated with a
slower breathing rate. Physical effects accompany a slower respiratory rate, including a decreased heart rate, decreased
metabolism, decreased fatigue, and decreased sympathetic nervous system functioning. This mind-body-breath connection
has only recently been acknowledged by Western science, but
the yogis of ancient times knew about it thousands of years
ago. The many different breathing techniques that they developed help us fasten our attention on the breath, shift our
breathing patterns, and in this way learn to influence our own
mind states.

To properly learn pranayama, you need to work with a qual-
ified teacher of yoga or Ayurveda. Many different aspects of the
breath can be explored, and a good teacher will be able to skillfully guide you in learning the various breathing patterns and
understanding which will be most useful to you under which
circumstances. Nonetheless, you may want to investigate a few
breathing techniques on your own, and some of these are
described below.

To begin, you want to make sure that you have a clean, well-ventilated room. (You can always practice pranayama outside, as long as you're breathing good, clean air.) Then get into a comfortable seated position. It's important that your position is comfortable enough that you can maintain it for a while: that way you won't be distracted by aches and pains in the body. Experiment until you find what works for you. If you can, sit in a cross-legged position on the floor. If your hips are tight and you find that your knees are higher than your hips, you'll definitely want to give yourself some extra lift. Try sitting on the edge of a blanket, pillow, or zafu (meditation pillow) until your knees drop down to at least the height of the hips. That way your spine will be supported to be more upright, and you won't have to make an effort to stay in this position.

When you are doing pranayama, you never want to force your breath. So if your nostrils are blocked, you don't want to push the breath in and out through the nose. Also, if you have problems with your eyes or ears, or if you are pregnant, you'll want to avoid holding the breath. Similarly, if you have heart problems or high blood pressure, don't hold your breath. If you find that you get dizzy or light-headed, just stop and return to a normal breath.

You may want to begin with a very simple practice in which you simply direct your attention to your breath, without trying to manipulate it in any way. Notice the movement of the breath just below the nostrils, above the upper lip. Can you tell which nostril is more open? (Usually one nostril dominates for about ninety minutes, and then this dominance switches to the other nostril.) Then see if you can feel the breath in other parts of the body. The breath is usually most easily detected in the chest. Observe the rise and fall of the chest as you breathe in and out. Then see if you can sense the breath elsewhere in the body. You may have the impression at first that the breath doesn't create movement in other parts of the body. Just go back to where you can discern movement, and keep your focus there. After working with this practice for a time, you'll find that you become more sensitive to the subtler sensations of the breath throughout the body. Try working with this practice for five minutes at a time, gradually increasing it to ten or fifteen minutes.

Ujjayi. If you find it too abstract to watch your breath in the way described above, you may prefer a practice that involves actively directing the breath. Ujjayi breathing is one of the most commonly used breaths in yoga practice, and it is also a wonderful practice in and of itself. For this breath, you intentionally close the throat very slightly, so that the air makes a soft sound as it passes through your throat, rather like wind going through a tunnel. The sound gives your mind something to concentrate on, and when your mind strays, you'll find that the sound becomes irregular or even disappears entirely. If this happens, just start again. Gradually, ujjayi breathing will feel more natural, and you will find that your breath automatically begins to be more deep and even.

Bhastrika. Take a breath in, and then exhale quickly and strongly. You'll want to emphasize the exhalation, strongly engaging the abdominal muscles to move the air out of the body, and then just let the breath come back in of its own accord. This is a more rapid breath: take about a second for each exhalation. Try ten repetitions at a time, and then take a few resting breaths, noting how you feel. This breath can be particularly useful to Kapha types, as it builds the capacity of the lungs and can help relieve asthma and some allergies. It's a warming breath that can benefit Vata types, too.

Shitali. For this breath, you'll curl your tongue into a tubelike shape and let it stick out slightly from your mouth. (If you cannot curl your tongue, then just let your tongue rest lightly against your top and bottom teeth, allowing enough space for air to pass over your tongue.) Then breathe in slowly through the tongue; pause at the top of your inhalation and hold the breath very briefly; then let the breath out through the nose. Try ten or so cycles of this breath. You'll notice that it has a cooling effect that you can feel immediately in the mouth. This breath is particularly useful for Pitta types.

Nadi shodhana. This breath involves breathing first through one nostril and then the other. Take your left hand up to your face, and use your pinky and ring fingers to block off the right nostril. Then slowly breathe out through your left nostril. Keep your fingers in the same position, and breathe in slowly through the left nostril. Then change your hand position so that your left thumb blocks off the left nostril. Breathe out slowly through the right nostril. Keep your fingers in the same position, and breathe in slowly through the right nostril. This constitutes one cycle. Try doing about ten cycles of this breath at a time. If you find that your left arm gets tired, then switch arms and use your right hand instead.

Nadi shodhana is one of the most important breathing exercises used in Ayurveda, as it balances Vata, Pitta, and Kapha. It also balances the two hemispheres of the brain: as you breathe through the left nostril, the right brain is stimulated, and as you use the right nostril, the left side of the brain is stimulated. In Ayurveda, these two sides of the brain correspond with the female and male energies, and by equally activating these two energies, you create balance between them.

Pranayama practices can be very powerful, and you will feel their effects quickly, particularly if you work with one or more of these practices on a regular basis. You may want to try to do a little pranayama every day for a week or two and observe how you feel. These practices, as well as shavasana, are meditations in and of themselves, though they are also meant to be preparations for deeper states of meditation. Still another practice that can help prepare the mind for meditation is the use of mantra.

MANTRA

Mantra involves the repetition of a sound. A mantra can be a syllable, a word, or even a whole verse. Traditionally, it is given to a student by a teacher, who has chosen the mantra based on the needs of the student. The mantra has a special meaning, and often it is used in conjunction with some sort of imagery. Some mantras are used to invoke a particular god or goddess; some are used to awaken certain parts of the body; others are used for particular healing purposes. When a mantra is practiced properly, in the way it was taught to the student, it is said to be an effective and powerful way to focus the mind.

Many mantras exist; the best known and most important is the mantra *om*. Om is the sound that is heard during deep meditation, and you can imitate this sound by chanting it aloud. Particularly if you are someone who is drawn to sound, and if you like to sing, you may want to try this mantra on your own and see how it affects you.

Om consists of the sounds "a" (ah), "u" (oo), and "m." When you chant om, the idea is to make the sound extend as long as you can, without straining. Start by taking a deep breath in, and then with the mouth fairly open, tone the sound "a." Gradually begin to narrow your mouth so that the sound evolves into more of a "u." Continue narrowing your mouth until your lips are closed, and let the humming sound continue through your closed lips. When you have run out of air, pause for a moment, then start again. Try doing this for five minutes. Then either sit quietly or lie down in shavasana, and take a few moments to register how this practice affects you.

MEDITATION

Meditation has been shown to have essentially the same benefits to both the mind and the body that pranayama does. Specific meditation practices may be prescribed to treat certain diseases and conditions, especially if there is a strong psychological component involved, and usually some form of meditation is recommended as part of an Ayurvedic program.

There are many different methods for meditating, and not every style of practice will necessarily work for you. Also, one way of meditating may work for a while, and then it becomes appropriate to change your practice. Meditation should really be learned under the guidance of a teacher, but until you find such a teacher, you may want, on your own, to try a few non-traditional techniques for quieting the mind.

A couple of different techniques are described below that I have found particularly helpful. Bear in mind, however, that these are just tools to use in order to create favorable conditions for a meditative state. Ultimately, any techiques, which are a bit like road maps, will fall away, and you'll find yourself at times in a true state of meditation in which the mind feels open and clear. During these moments, you may experience a sense of space or expansion or freedom. It is, of course, delightful when we experience such inner openings, but they don't always happen so easily. That is why we have the practices: so that we can turn back to them when the need arises and cultivate our concentration again. What will also help you, whatever way you choose to meditate, is to be rooted in an Ayurvedic lifestyle; all of the healthy lifestyle choices that you make will support your meditation practice.

Just as with pranayama, when you meditate, you'll want to be in a clean, well-ventilated room. (Again, you can be outside, too, if that suits you.) Especially if you are serious about trying to make meditation a regular part of your life, you may want to set aside a whole room for your practice (if you have that much space in your home). If that is not an option, then you may want to just create a special area for yourself. Some people like to set up an altar of some kind. You can make your altar any way you like, decorating it with any images or objects that are meaningful to you and that will support you in stilling and clearing your mind. Some people like to have a picture of their teacher or a statue of a deity; others like to keep it simple and have fresh flowers or seashells or something that reminds them of nature.

Wherever you meditate, choose a relatively quiet place, and try to minimize the chances of being interrupted. (It's a good idea to turn off phone ringers and lower the volume of answering machines.) Then make sure that you are warm enough. You may want to drape a light blanket or shawl around you so that you don't get cold. Find a comfortable seated position, giving yourself whatever extra support you need in the way of blankets or pillows so that you'll be able to maintain this position easily for fifteen or twenty minutes. Again, that means that when you sit cross-legged, your knees should not come higher than your hips; in fact, it's better if the knees are a little lower than your hips. By all means, use a chair if sitting cross-legged doesn't work for you. In the beginning, you may find that you'll need to experiment a little more to find a position that you can easily maintain. If, while you're meditating, you are overly distracted by uncomfortable or painful sensations in your body, then go ahead and shift your position so that you are more comfortable. After a few sessions, you'll have a better sense of how exactly you need to position yourself so that you won't have to keep readjusting.

Feeling stillness. Once you are set up, take a few moments to direct your attention to your breath, just watching the breath as it moves in and out of the body. (If your mind is in a more restless state, you may find it useful to do some of the prana-yama practices first.) See if you can observe the breath without directing it. Let it settle into a natural rhythm. Then, as your breathing becomes more settled and as the mind quiets down, begin to pay more attention to the points of transition in your breathing. When you reach the top of your inhalation, notice the slight pause that occurs before the breath begins to move out of your body. Similarly, when you reach the bottom of your exhalation, observe the pause before your breath comes back in. Over time, what you will become aware of is a kind of still point as the breath transitions; it's a moment where time seems almost to be suspended. Don't be dismayed if it takes a little while to begin to feel this. Try the practice a few times, and notice how you are affected. You may want to try sitting for just ten minutes initially and then gradually build up to fifteen or twenty minutes.

Who am I? Start as above, by directing your attention to your breath. Allow yourself several minutes in which to become more aware of the natural movement of the breath in your body. Then, when your mind feels more open and quiet, ask yourself the question, "Who am I?" You may be tempted to answer in words to yourself, but instead, see if you can just stay with whatever sensations and feelings arise in response to the question. As you proceed, you will likely find your attention straying, and thoughts will come into your mind. As soon as you become aware of thinking, ask yourself, "Who is thinking?" Then repeat the question, "Who am I?" The idea is not to answer the question with the rational mind but to repeatedly and patiently asking the question, immersing yourself in a non-rational awareness of your Self. This practice takes time. Try it for a shorter period of time, like ten minutes, and then see if you can do it for longer.

Know that with any meditation practice, it isn't always easy; obstacles of one sort or another will inevitably arise. That is why we have teachers to help us. It can also be tremendously helpful to meditate with a group, especially when you are starting out. That way, you have the energy of the group to support your efforts as well as the company of other people to share experiences with.

Some yoga classes offer meditation as part of the class, though typically meditation is given minimal time. However, a few yoga studios do offer ongoing meditation classes, so you may want to check around at any nearby yoga studios. If you are working with an Ayurvedic practitioner, he or she will probably be able to direct you as well.

Though you may not realize it, color can strongly affect how you think and feel. Certainly, this is something that designers of advertisements are well aware of: colors are selected very carefully, with the express intent of stimulating consumers into buying more.

How color therapy works is fairly commonsense: once you have an idea of which colors are most appropriate for your type, you can begin to surround yourself with those colors. You may want to paint the interior of your home or workplace with these colors, or make a point of dressing in these colors. You can also use colored light bulbs or shades in your home, or you can stretch colored paper across your windows to color the light that floods into your rooms. You can even infuse water with the vibration of color by letting water stand in a colored glass container in the sunlight for a few hours; then, when you drink the water, you absorb the healing properties of the color. You can also meditate on colors that appear in nature, like the blue of the sky or the green of trees and plants. In addition, if you are able to visualize, you can envision a color in your mind and then surround yourself, or a particular body part, with that color.

Vatas and Color

Vata types tend to be cold, dry, and overly nervous and active. So selecting colors that have opposite qualities—warmth, moisture, calmness—will be most therapeutic. Vatas do best with warm colors like red, gold, yellow, and orange. It is important, however, that these colors not be too bright, as brighter colors can actually be deranging to Vatas. Other colors that can be balancing are light greens and blues and soft cream colors. Colors that are dark may deplete Vatas, and purple in particular may be aggravating. Though Vatas usually benefit from having more color around them, they need to be careful that the colors are not too strongly contrasting with one another, as this can be aggravating.

Pittas and Color

Pittas tend to be hot, moist, and sharp, so they will want to steer clear of red, orange, and yellow colors, as well as any colors that are very bright. Generally, less color is better for Pittas: the colors that they do surround themselves with should be cooling and calming. Pastel shades, gray colors, or more natural and neutral colors are the most balancing. Greens, blues, and whites can also be appropriate.

Kaphas and Color

To counteract their sedentary tendencies, Kaphas need colors that are stimulating. They also need colors that are warming and drying. The best colors for Kaphas are bright colors like reds, golds, oranges, and yellows. Colors that are too saturated and dark are aggravating to Kaphas; similarly, colors that are too mild, like many pastel colors, are aggravating. Cool colors in the blue and green families should also be avoided.

GEM THERAPY AND MINERAL AND METAL THERAPY

Gem, mineral, and metal therapies are much too involved to go into in this book, but they do bear mentioning, as they are an important piece of the Ayurvedic tradition.

Traditionally, certain metals and minerals are used in special preparations that are taken internally; some of the metals and minerals used are copper, gold, silver, iron, tin, mica, lead, sulfur, and mercury. The preparations can be elaborate, or they can be fairly simple, and they have specific actions on the body and mind. For instance, a preparation might have an impact on a particular organ of the body, or it might have an antibacterial effect, or it might be useful for balancing a certain dosha. If you are interested in learning more about this aspect of Ayurveda, Vasant Lad's book *The Complete Book of Ayurvedic Home Remedies* is a good place to start. Any kind of deeper investigation will require consulting with an Ayurvedic practitioner.

Gems and precious stones are also used for their healing properties. Just as minerals and metals have specific effects, gems and stones do, too. Typically, they are worn on the body as jewelry, either as rings or necklaces. Ayurveda provides definite guidelines as to the size of the gems, and which kinds of gems and stones should be worn on which fingers in order to produce the optimal effect. It is also possible to absorb the healing properties of these gems and stones by soaking them in water for a period of time and then drinking the water. Again, Vasant Lad's book *The Complete Book of Ayurvedic Home Remedies* provides some specific information on this part of Ayurveda.

AROMATHERAPY

One of the supplementary therapies used in Ayurveda is aromatherapy. Although smell is the least developed of our senses, most of us recognize the remarkable power that smell can have over our moods. In an instant, smell can transport us to some other time in our lives, leaving us with a vague sense of familiarity. Or, more startlingly, a smell can suddenly thrust a buried memory up into our consciousness. Smell can also call to mind a particular person or place. Whatever the sense of smell evokes, it can be either pleasant or disturbing, soothing or stimulating. Not surprisingly, then, we can learn to use smell as an adjunct to other Ayurvedic practices to help cultivate a more balanced state of mind.

Aromatherapy can be used in different forms. Most of us are familiar with incense; incense is usually made from plant material, like the bark or sap of different kinds of trees, or it can be specially processed from certain oils. Often, incense is just one scent, but sometimes several scents are combined to create an aromatic mix. Incense is usually burned directly, though some types require a piece of charcoal for burning the incense on. Also, some incense creates just a thin ribbon of smoke, while others burn more heavily, making the air denser. Some varieties are very strong in smell and can be overpowering; others are lighter and more delicate and exert a subtler effect. What sort of incense to use and how to use it varies from person to person and depends on your dosha, your present state of mind, and your personal preferences.

For a Vata type, you may want to steer clear of scents that are too strong or stimulating. Remember that Vatas tend toward fear and anxiety, so selecting a sweet scent, like rose, that is more calming and restorative may be appropriate for you. If your dosha is Pitta, you will want to choose "cooler" smells to dampen the excessive fire of Pitta; these include scents like lavender and gardenia. Kapha types require more stimulating smells to help them overcome their tendency toward inertia; such scents could include frankincense or musk.

To more completely take in the smell, you can directly breathe in the incensed air. If you have an altar, or some special place where you like to meditate, you may want to incorporate the burning of incense into your meditation, allowing yourself to take in the smell as you simultaneously cultivate a more relaxed, open state of mind. If you just want to create a more general effect, you can burn incense in different parts of your home. Another way to use a favorite incense is to place a box of incense in one of your drawers so that your clothes gradually soak in the aroma. If you are at all inclined to use incense, take the time to experiment until you find a few that really work for you; using incense can be most healing to the nervous system and the mind.

Aromatherapy can also involve the use of essential oils. An essential oil is just what it sounds like: the essence, in a concentrated oil form, of a particular plant. Because essential oils are so concentrated, they are very potent and are therefore inappropriate for internal use unless properly diluted; in fact, some essential oils can be damaging if accidentally ingested in their pure form or if they come into contact with delicate areas like the eyes. So never take these oils internally unless you have clear instructions about how exactly to use them!

Essential oils can be sniffed directly from their bottles; a drop or two of oil can be mixed well into a bath; or a small drop can also be applied directly to particular points on the body. An obvious place is the wrists, where many of us are accustomed to dabbing perfume. When an essential oil is placed on the wrist, it's easy to take in a whiff from time to time. You could also place a drop on the ankles or knees; other possibilities include specific points on the body, called marmas, that are comparable to acupuncture points used in Chinese medicine. Though we may be less aware of the smell of the oils when applied on these points, the fiery, penetrating nature of oils can actually work more deeply, actually affecting organ systems in the body and in that way facilitating the flow of prana, our life energy. There are hundreds of these points, and some of the more important that might be used in aromatherapy are at the heart, the navel, and on the back.

This chapter has covered several different Ayurvedic practices that you can begin to incorporate into your life. You may be wondering, though, how best to fit all of these things into your routine. In the next chapter, you will find specific recommendations for how to try shaping your daily life to make optimal use of Ayurveda's methods.

seven

STAYING HEALTHY WITH
AN AYURVEDIC ROUTINE

Ayurveda places a great deal of emphasis on prevention of disease. So rather than waiting until there is a problem, you can begin to strengthen your whole system and bolster your immunity now by integrating the practices of Ayurveda into your life. In the Ayurvedic view, our health depends on our living in tune with the cycles of nature. We also need to live in accord with our *own* nature by taking into account our constitution as we make choices about how to live. The best way to do this is through establishing appropriate and regular daily routines. If we don't have regular, healthy habits, and we allow ourselves to become erratic in our sleeping, eating, or exercise patterns, then we are more likely to experience disturbances in the doshas, which then affect our well-being as a whole.

No doubt you have already experienced what happens when your habits are irregular: when you get too much or too little sleep, you don't function as well. Eating too much rich food or too late at night can leave you feeling poorly. Too little exercise or the wrong kind of exercise can similarly upset your sense of equilibrium. The idea, then, is to try to create a healthy daily routine that you can stick to most of the time. Once you have established a routine that really works for you, then you'll find that your whole system works more efficiently, and you won't be as negatively affected by those little deviations from your routine that are bound to occur from time to time.

PACING YOURSELF

As you read through these suggestions, you may feel overwhelmed by how much there is to do. Bear in mind that self-care *does* take time and effort. Your reward will be that you feel better and stay healthier—and in the long run, if you can avoid getting sick in the first place, you will, in fact, be freer to use your time and energy as you wish.

As you're considering making changes in your lifestyle, try to be aware of how much change you can tolerate at once. Some of us do well throwing ourselves wholeheartedly into a new program and making several changes at a time, while for others this approach can be counterproductive. It all depends on you and how you generally cope with change. Always be patient with yourself. Try to commit yourself to a practice for a certain period of time, and notice how you feel as a result. If you feel better, then obviously you will be motivated to continue. If you don't feel better, then it's possible that you may need a longer period of adjustment, or perhaps you need to slightly change what it is that you're doing. You may need to just focus on some other aspect of your routine for a while. Avoid the trap of becoming too rigid with yourself, and allow yourself some flexibility. For the purposes of tracking exactly what you're doing and watching your responses, you may find it useful to buy a journal and make regular entries of what you've done each day.

THE DAILY ROUTINE

According to Ayurveda, the days go through two cycles in which Vata, Pitta, and Kapha alternately dominate. From about 6:00 to 10:00 A.M. the Kapha dosha is dominant. From 10:00 A.M. to 2:00 P.M. the Pitta dosha takes over; from 2:00 to 6:00 P.M. the Vata dosha is in control. Then the cycle repeats itself: Kapha takes over again, dominating from about 6:00 P.M. to 10:00 P.M. Pitta is dominant from 10:00 P.M. to 2:00 A.M., and Vata once more takes over from 2:00 to 6:00 A.M. Your daily activities should take into account these naturally occurring rhythms. In this way, you optimize your physical, mental, and spiritual health.

Ayurveda traditionally recommends getting up early, before the sun rises, during the Vata-dominated time, when the Vata qualities of lightness, movement, and clarity are present. Kapha people, who need the least amount of sleep of all the types, should get up the earliest, around 4:30. Pitta people should aim for about 5:30. And Vata types, who tend to need more sleep, can sleep in until 6:00 or so.

These are ideal times and are not necessarily practical for everyone: just do the best that you can. Bear in mind that the longer you sleep into the Kapha time that follows (after 6:00), the more you may feel Kapha qualities of heaviness and dullness.

Suggested Morning Routines

Many of the routines that follow are based on those recommended in various books, including Lad's *The Complete Book of Ayurvedic Home Remedies* and Anselmo's *Ayurvedic Secrets to Longevity and Total Health*.

• One of the first things to do when you get up is to drink a glass of lukewarm water. (Make sure that the water is not cold, and if you are a Vata or Kapha type, you may even want to warm the water slightly.) Drinking water helps to flush out your kidneys and will also stimulate your bowels.

• Empty your bladder and, if you can, your bowels. (Regular bowel movements are an important part of health, so try to get in the habit if you aren't already.)

• Clean your teeth and tongue. For the teeth, you can use a soft toothbrush. You can use Ayurvedic toothpastes and powders, which can usually be found in health food stores. Before you clean your tongue, take a good look at it in the mirror. Notice if there is much of a coating; if there is, you have excess ama, or toxins, in your system. (If you're not sure what constitutes a lot of coating, just keep checking every day; after a while, you'll have more of a sense of what your tongue normally looks like, and it will be easier to detect excessive coating.) To clean the tongue, you can use the edge of a spoon, gently scraping from the back of the tongue forward, about ten times. What works slightly better is to use a tongue scraper, which you can also find at many health food stores.

• To help keep the mouth clean and prevent diseases of the gums, you can gargle with sesame oil. You can also gently massage the gums with sesame oil.

• Give yourself a full body massage. (See instructions in chapter 5.) If you don't have time to give yourself a full fifteen minutes, just take four or five minutes. After your massage, take a bath or shower.

• Exercise according to your type. Walking can be a wonderful way to begin the day, as it not only exercises your body but also can put you in touch with nature, especially if you walk in a natural setting. Yoga is also recommended for all the types. If you already practice yoga, you may want to modify your practice, keeping in mind the suggestions that are given in chapter 5. If you are new to yoga, then you'll want a more thorough introduction. You can begin with *Simple Yoga,* which includes guidelines for finding classes and teachers.

• After your exercise, practice a little pranayama. If you have the time, then try two or more of the breathing practices. Otherwise, simply work with one breathing pattern that is suitable for your type. (See chapter 6.)

• After your pranayama practice, you can do a little meditation, following guidelines given in chapter 6 if you don't already have a meditation practice.

• Have your breakfast after you've completed the above routines. Vata and Pitta types should definitely eat breakfast, but for Kaphas it may be more beneficial to skip breakfast entirely.

DAY

Having completed your morning routines, you'll be ready to head off to your work, whatever that is. Keep in mind that at about 10:00 A.M., Pitta begins to dominate; Pitta powers the intellect, so you may find it useful to capitalize on increased mental capacity at this time of day.

The Nature of Your Work

Here, it is also worth briefly discussing the kind of work that you do. If you derive real satisfaction from your work, then you are probably doing exactly what you need to be doing at the moment. If, on the other hand, you do not feel happy with your work, then it could be that you are doing work that is inappropriate for your type.

Take Dan, for instance, who is a predominantly Pitta type. Dan worked as a carpenter, which, for many years, satisfied his need to make beautiful, finely crafted cabinetry for people's homes. When he moved to the South, he found that the stifling heat of the summer, combined with a growing boredom with the repetitive nature of carpentry, made him less and less enthusiastic about his work. Dan finally recognized that laboring in the intense heat was extremely draining to him; he also realized that he needed to make better use of his intellect. Dan went back to school and studied to become an architect. This allowed him to keep his hand in the world of aesthetics and to feel that he was making better use of his talents; at the same time, the change removed him from the more grueling physical work that had begun to drain his body, especially in the summer. He is now a much happier, more balanced person. (He continues to do carpentry but for his own personal pleasure.)

Because work makes up such a large part of our lives, it's important that we do work that is satisfying and nourishing and that makes the best use of our innate gifts. If you are unhappy with your work life, you may need to carefully examine your situation, taking into account the natural talents and strengths that go along with your type as well as your areas of weakness.

Handling Stress at Work

Whatever the nature of your work, your days are bound to have some stress in them. Some people's jobs are, of course, more stressful than others', but whatever the degree of stress that you deal with on a daily basis, what is important is how you handle stressful situations as they arise.

As you integrate more Ayurvedic practices into your life, you'll find that you automatically handle stress more skillfully: things that may have previously produced strong reactions in you will simply not bother you as much, and you'll have more capacity to maintain a sense of calm throughout the events of your day. However, you may still encounter some very challenging situations, and at times you may want to bring some of your practices into the workplace.

Stress can produce an elevated heart rate, perspiration, anxiety, anger, and other unpleasant reactions. If you find yourself reacting in these ways, you may want to try taking some time out—even for just five minutes—to help calm yourself. If you have the luxury of a private office, you can close your door and practice some of the cooling breathing techniques or relaxing meditations that are described in chapter 6. If you don't have any privacy in your workplace, then retreating to the bathroom can be an alternative; you can take a few slow and deep breaths in the privacy of the bathroom stall. Getting up and taking a quick walk is another option. Even if you are in a situation that you can't get away from immediately, like a trying conversation with a difficult boss or client, you can still make it a point to take a few mindful breaths in the moment. Initially, you may have trouble remembering to pay attention to your breath, but as the breathing patterns become more familiar and feel more natural during your morning routine, you'll have an easier time including them in the rest of your day.

Suggested Afternoon Routines

• At noon is when Pitta peaks, making your digestion particularly strong, so you'll want to be sure to eat your lunch at about this time. It's recommended that Vatas eat somewhere between 11:00 A.M. and noon; Pitta types should eat at noon; and Kaphas can eat a little later, between noon and 1:00 P.M. Because the digestive fire is so strong at this time of day, you should make lunch your biggest meal. Follow the guidelines for your constitution, and include a few sips of warm water with your meal to improve your digestion. Avoid the temptation to use your lunch break to catch up on reading, mail, and other tasks that may be calling to you. This way, you reserve your body's energy for eating, and your meal will be better digested. To further aid the digestive process, you may want to take a brief walk after lunch.

• From 2:00 to 6:00 P.M. is when the Vata dosha dominates. That means that you may want to use these hours for more creative, visionary work.

• Your transition from work back to home is a time that you can use to unwind and de-stress. If you live reasonably close to work, then you may want to consider walking to or from work if you aren't already doing so. That may add time to your commute, but the therapeutic benefits can make it worthwhile. If doing this every day is too much, then perhaps you could make it a point to walk once a week.

If you don't have the option of walking and have to commute by train, bus, or car, then you may want to consider using that time slightly differently. If you're commuting by train or bus, you can use your commute, or a portion of it, to practice pranayama or meditation. If you are travelling by car, you may want to minimize listening to the radio; so much of radio airtime is taken up with jarring advertisements that you'll have a harder time relaxing and focusing inward if you subject yourself to too much. Instead, you can make a point of listening to cassettes or CDs of calming music.

NIGHT

At about 6:00 P.M., day shifts into night, and Vata gives way to Kapha. A natural winding-down begins to happen at this hour.

Suggested Evening Routines

• Dinner should generally be eaten between 6:00 and 7:00 P.M., preferably closer to 6:00 if you can. Eating dinner much later is not recommended, as it may disrupt your sleep. Also, many people are used to eating their largest meal at dinner, but doing so can actually cause stomachaches and acidity and can also tax your digestion. Therefore, you should keep this meal relatively light, especially if you are a Kapha type. (Pittas may sometimes need to eat a more substantial dinner.) To aid your digestion, you may want to take a brief walk after your meal.

• Evenings can be spent as you wish. Steer clear of TV programs or movies that are overly stimulating, as these can disturb your sleep.

• If you have the time, take a few moments to give yourself another massage before retiring. (If you are concerned about getting oil on your bed sheets, then you can either shower immediately after your massage or use a minimal amount of oil.)

• Before you go to bed, you may want to spend a few minutes reading something of a meditative nature. You can also take a few minutes to actually meditate. This will help you unwind a bit more and will make your sleep more restful and restorative.

• It's recommended that you go to bed around 10:00 P.M. (If you stay up much later, then you will be entering the Pitta phase of night, which goes from 10:00 P.M. to 2:00 A.M., and you may find yourself getting a second wind and staying up later than is truly good for you.) Vatas need the most sleep and should generally be in bed by 10:00 P.M. Pittas can go to bed a little later, somewhere between 10:00 P.M. and 11:00 P.M. Though they may be more inclined to retire early, Kaphas can actually stay up quite a bit later, until somewhere between 11:00 P.M. and midnight; this way, they won't oversleep, which is their tendency.

SEASONAL SHIFTS IN YOUR ROUTINE

Once you have established certain routines in your life, you'll want to remain open to making slight adjustments to these in order to compensate for the changes that occur in the seasons. Of course, as you're thinking about how to make these modifications, you also need to take into account how drastic those seasonal shifts are. In some locations, the change of seasons is dramatic, and if you live in such a place, you may need to make more modifications. In other locations the seasonal changes are much more subtle, and you may not need to be as concerned about modifying your routine. As you read, you'll see that the kinds of adjustments you'll want to make are quite commonsense.

Fall and Winter

The Vata dosha tends to dominate during the fall and winter. This covers the time period from about October through February, or perhaps a little later, depending on where you live. During this time, you can observe an increase of many Vata qualities in the natural environment: the days grow shorter and cooler; plants dry up and lose their leaves; it gets windier, and the air can have a more brittle feeling. These environmental changes can make you more prone to Vata-related disorders, and you will be even more vulnerable if you are a Vata type. Below are a few things you can do to protect yourself.

• Be especially mindful about staying regular in your routines: an erratic schedule will tend to throw Vata out of balance.

• Emphasize foods that will help to pacify Vata. Eat more warm, oily, and heavy foods, and try to increase your intake of foods that are sweet, sour, or salty. Stay away from foods that are dry, light, and cold. Add more warm drinks to your diet.

• As the air gets cooler, make sure to bundle up for warmth and for protection against the wind. In your wardrobe, you may want to emphasize colors that are Vata pacifying, like red, gold, yellow, and orange.

• Don't overdo your exercise, especially if you are a Vata type. You may also want to cut down on outdoor exercise, particularly if you are a Vata.

• Get plenty of rest. You may want to allow yourself occasional naps, should you feel the need.

Spring

From about March through May, the Kapha dosha becomes more dominant. With the coming of spring, you'll see some Kapha qualities reflected in nature, particularly the moisture that comes with the melting of snow and the sweetness that begins to fill the air as plants begins blooming. People often find themselves more susceptible to Kapha problems during the spring, like allergies, colds, sinus congestion, and flus, but these can be circumvented or more easily managed by taking Kapha-reducing measures.

• Continue to eat warm foods; drink hot drinks. Steer clear of cold foods and drinks as well as dairy products: all of these aggravate Kapha. Shift your emphasis away from sweet, sour, and salty foods, and begin eating more bitter, astringent, and pungent foods. You can begin to eat more lightly, especially if you are a Kapha type.

• Adjust your wardrobe, wearing warm clothes (and emphasizing Kapha-pacifying colors like red, gold, orange, and yellow) until you feel the need to begin shedding layers as spring advances.

• Avoid oversleeping, particularly if you are a Kapha type. Make a special effort to get up before 6:00 A.M., when the Kapha cycle of the day begins.

Summer

The long days of summer can be especially bright and hot, both qualities of the Pitta dosha, which rules this season. Health problems that afflict people at this time of year, such as rashes, skin inflammation, or sunburn, are often related to high, or aggravated, Pitta. To lower your chances of Pitta-related problems, follow some of the Pitta-reducing measures listed below.

• Particularly if you live in an unusually warm place, then you'll want to make every effort to keep yourself cool. Avoid being directly in the sun, and try to stay inside during the middle of the day when it tends to be hottest. If you have to be outside, then cover your head and use sunglasses to shade and protect your eyes.

• Follow a Pitta-reducing diet that emphasizes cooling foods. Bring into your diet more sweet, bitter, and astringent tastes; avoid sour, salty, and pungent tastes. Don't drink hot drinks; instead, have cold drinks. (Don't use ice, however, as this can interfere with your digestion.)

• Wear clothes made from light fabrics that breathe easily; emphasize colors that are cooling, like greens, blues, whites, grays, and pastel shades.

• Adjust your exercise routine so that you exercise only during the cooler parts of the day. You may want to cut back on your exercise during these hotter months; you may also want to add swimming to your routine, as this can help the body throw off excess heat.

Once you begin to bring these routines into your life, you'll want to give yourself ample time to fine-tune them and get used to them. When you've integrated them into your life in a way that is really right for you, the benefits will be clear, and you may even discover that living this way feels more natural and easy and ultimately requires less energy than what you were doing before.

eight

AYURVEDA FOR WOMEN

The biology of women is drastically different from that of men. This distinction becomes obvious when a girl reaches puberty and begins menstruating. The monthly hormonal cycle then becomes a part of her life and can last for many years, until she enters menopause.

HORMONE CYCLES

Some women are able to sail through their monthly cycles relatively trouble free. It seems, though, that many women in this culture experience difficulty—whether mild or extreme—with their periods. The majority of women suffer from PMS at some point in their lives; also, a large percentage experience uncomfortable or painful menstruation.

Ayurveda understands that, like other health problems, difficulties with the menstrual cycle are caused by an imbalance in the doshas. The Vata, Pitta, and Kapha doshas are responsible for certain aspects of your cycle and, when out of balance, produce particular kinds of symptoms. It's important to understand that you may have an imbalance in any one of these doshas, regardless of what your type is. For instance, a Vata woman may have Vata-related menstrual problems, but she could just as easily have problems that are caused by Pitta or Kapha imbalances. If your menstrual cycle is in any way problematic, the descriptions below may give you a clue as to which dosha is responsible. You may also find that your symptoms correspond with two doshas or even all three.

Vata

When Vata is out of balance, the menstrual cycle can become irregular, or it can be unusually long. Menstruation can be preceded or accompanied by mood swings, feelings of insecurity or anxiety, nervous tension, and insomnia. Blood flow may be light, and it may be darker in color and contain some clots. Cramping, lower-back pain, and joint pain are common. There may be abdominal discomfort and bloating as well as constipation.

Pitta

For women who have Pitta imbalance, periods may still be regular, but they can come closer together. Before menstruation, there may be strong food cravings and increased appetite, feelings of irritability and anger, and acne or other irritations of the skin. Menstruation can come with headaches, diarrhea, hot flashes, and feelings of too much body heat. Blood flow is heavy and lasts longer; the blood is usually a bright red color.

Kapha

With Kapha imbalance, the cycle is regular and is often accompanied by bloating and weight gain. Breasts can be swollen and tender. There can be achiness and stiffness in the joints and back. Feelings of lethargy, sleepiness, and depression are common. Blood flow can be heavy and there may be clotting; blood is a lighter color.

Tips for Balancing Your Cycle

If your symptoms seem to be related to imbalances in more than one dosha, your situation is a little more complex and may require more measures than are suggested here. Particularly if you have extreme symptoms, you'll want to consult with an Ayurvedic practitioner who can prescribe more specific measures, including herbal formulas. In any case, the self-care tips listed below will certainly not be harmful and will probably help.

Rest. Unfortunately, most women in our culture do not take the time to rest and care for themselves as they should during their menses. Our culture simply does not support doing so, though in many other places in the world, including India, it is quite common for menstruating women to retreat from their normal duties and allow other household members to take up the slack. Peter Anselmo points out in his book *Ayurvedic Secrets to Longevity and Total Health* that Ayurveda actually views a woman's cycle as an opportunity for cleansing and rejuvenation. Taking time to rest is, in fact, one of the most beneficial things you can do for yourself. With each monthly cycle, enormous hormonal shifts take place in your body, and it is not only reasonable but also prudent to be aware of these changes and make adjustments accordingly.

In order to rest more, you need to give some thought as to how to reorganize your life for a few days each month so that you'll have more time to rest. Some women make arrangements to work at home for a few days before or during their period. You may want to reorganize your work and household tasks in such a way that as your period approaches, you spend less time doing the more demanding aspects and more time doing the things that are easier. You can think ahead and arrange to have certain aspects of your life in order before your period starts so that those things are already taken care of. It can also be helpful to cut back on your socializing for a few days.

Diet and herbs. Wrong diet can be a cause of both PMS and menstrual problems. When your diet is poor, or inappropriate for your type, there will be a buildup of ama, or toxins, in your system. In Ayurveda, your period can be understood as the body's attempt to clean itself out, not just of the unused egg and the lining of your uterus, but also of the toxins that have built up in your body. If there is a lot of ama buildup in your system, your periods will be more difficult. Many menstrual difficulties can be avoided if you are already keeping your system clear of ama by following a diet that is appropriate for your type. You will also do best by cutting down on or even eliminating your consumption of alcohol, caffeine, sugar, and chocolate, as these are some of the major culprits in PMS.

You may also need to make a few other dietary adjustments. Suppose, for example, that you are a Vata type, but your menstrual symptoms are generally more of a Pitta nature. You might have a buildup of Pitta symptoms just before your period (like strong food cravings, headaches, and acne, for example). In such a case, as well as following your usual Vata-pacifying diet, you might want to try adding a few Pitta-reducing measures, too, especially as your period draws near and your symptoms flare up. You could try avoiding deep-fried, oily foods as well as foods that are spicy. It might also be helpful to stay away from certain dairy products, like butter and hard cheeses. Each person is unique, so you'll want to experiment a little to see what seems to work for you.

Many herbal formulas can help reduce menstrual discomfort. Best is to have the guidance of an Ayurvedic practitioner, but if you are interested in pursuing this aspect on your own, several formulas are included in Atreya's book *Ayurvedic Healing for Women*. Also, *The Complete Book of Ayurvedic*

Home Remedies, by Vasant Lad, includes a few simple formulas. One preventative measure that he recommends for all types is to take a single tablespoon of aloe vera gel, three times a day, for the entire week preceding your period.

Modify exercise and yoga routines. It is normal to feel less inclined to continue your usual exercise routine when you are menstruating or about to start menstruating. If your body gives you signals that it wants to slow down, then listen, and make adjustments. You may want to cut back on what you usually do or try something different. For instance, if you are a runner, it may be more therapeutic for you to do some brisk walking (instead of running) for the few days before your period or during your period.

Regarding yoga practice: again, it is wise to make some changes to your usual routine. Do less, if that is what your body tells you it needs. You may find a few gentle stretches helpful, particularly if you have painful periods, but in general, you won't want to do a strong yoga practice. Also, for some women, it is best not to do any inverted poses (like headstand or handstand, in which the head is below the heart), as these poses can disrupt the flow of blood and can actually make menstruation painful and heavy.

Meditation, particularly during your period, is a practice that will reduce stress and can help alleviate some of the uncomfortable symptoms that may accompany menstruation. If you are not already meditating regularly, try at least giving yourself a few minutes for this practice before and during your period.

Implementing some of these changes may take some time, and it could be a little while before you fine-tune your program enough to get the full benefits. It's worth the effort, though. Some women find that once they figure out how best to manage their monthly cycle, they actually become aware of creative reservoirs in themselves that they can use and enjoy.

PREGNANCY

Ayurveda has a fair amount to say about the major, life-changing event of pregnancy. It is stressed that a woman should be in good health before becoming pregnant: this increases the chances of the baby being healthy and also makes pregnancy and delivery easier. In addition, the father should also be healthy, as it is the constitutions of both parents that determine the constitution of the child. Ideally, both parents undergo about a year-long program of purification and strengthening before they even try to conceive. Feelings of love and tenderness should be cultivated as much as possible during this time. Then, according to classical texts, an auspicious night is chosen for conception.

Of course, many pregnancies are not planned for, and parents are not necessarily in an optimal state of health either physically or emotionally when their child is conceived. However, health can always be improved upon. The main thing is to create and maintain the best possible environment for the growing fetus, as this very early influence is what will shape the child's character and development. A pregnant woman has an ongoing practice of becoming healthy and staying that way as much as possible through her diet, exercise habits, and other routines. It is especially helpful if she can decrease or eliminate any stressful influences around her. Below is a list of some of the things that Ayurveda emphasizes during pregnancy.

Tips for Pregnancy

Diet. Drugs, caffeine, and alcohol should be eliminated. Pregnancy is not a time to do any sort of detoxification (including panchakarma) or drastic dieting, as this can be too extreme. However, a healthy diet is very important. Because Vata tends to be high during pregnancy, you'll want to follow a diet that is somewhat Vata pacifying. Stay away from highly processed foods and foods that are frozen or canned; instead, bring into your diet plenty of fresh fruits and vegetables, fresh juices, whole grains, and milk. Eat regularly, and follow the cravings that your body has, as they can indicate a physical need for something in particular. Your body may need extra fluid intake, so make sure to drink plenty of water. Some herbs can be helpful during pregnancy, too, but you'll need to consult another book or work with an Ayurvedic practitioner for this information.

Exercise and yoga. Modify exercise routines as necessary. If you're a runner, you'll want to stop running at a certain point and switch to something that is less jarring, like swimming or walking. If you practice yoga, you'll need to make modifications as your pregnancy progresses. You may find that taking a prenatal yoga class is most beneficial, as the teacher can help you understand what kinds of modifications are appropriate. Whatever kind of exercise you do, always avoid straining.

Stress. Cut back on stressful influences in your life as much as you are able. Traditionally in India, a pregnant woman was given extra physical and emotional care and didn't have to venture outside the house during pregnancy. This is not practical for the majority of women, but you can still give thought to those stressful parts of your life that could maybe be set aside for this time period. Lighten your workload if you can, and enlist the support of other people—friends or family—as much as you can.

Rest. Give yourself adequate rest. If you can take naps, do so when you are inclined to. Extra rest is especially crucial during the first few months of pregnancy as well as in the eighth and ninth months.

Abhyanga and massage. Practice self-massage (abhyanga) on a daily basis. Give extra time to your belly, especially as it grows bigger: in addition to nourishing you, this may also help with stretch marks. If you can afford to get massages, do so as often as you can; your body can use any extra support it can get during this process. If you are suffering from certain discomforts that come along with pregnancy, like heartburn, sciatica, edema, or varicose veins, a good massage therapist will be able to work the appropriate marma points to help give you some relief.

Meditate. If you don't already have children, take advantage of the free quiet time that is still available to you; soon it will be much more difficult to find these precious moments. Meditation is an especially beneficial practice during pregnancy, as it will help you cope with stress and relax. Meditation is also an excellent preparation for childbirth.

Many other tips and practices will help ease your pregnancy. Especially if you have a particular uncomfortable symptom associated with pregnancy, Ayurveda suggests certain measures that you can take to improve the situation. Much of this information is available in books (see the sources in the back), but to get the most from Ayurveda during your pregnancy, you'll again want to consult with an Ayurvedic practitioner.

Menopause is another important milestone in a woman's later life. These more advanced years are dominated by the Vata dosha, so it is common to see symptoms that are associated with an increase in Vata: the body begins to shrink in size, becoming more dry and light; the skin gets thinner and dries up; hair can also thin out. Joints become stiffer, and there may be more of a tendency toward constipation. Being smaller and more thin-skinned makes people in the Vata stage of life more prone to getting cold. A few other symptoms that are especially associated with menopause are insomnia, headaches, hot flashes, mood swings, anxiety, depression, and memory loss.

Some positive Vata qualities may be more available to women during their menopausal years. Many women report that they feel more creative than ever. Some women also say that they feel more intuitive. This is a time when the expansive quality of Vata takes over, and a woman begins to turn more of her attention to the larger world of spirit.

How a woman goes through menopause is variable: some women sail through relatively quickly and easily, while for others the process is more drawn out and difficult. If you have been taking care of yourself up to the time of your Vata years, the chances of menopause being easier on you are greater. If you have neglected your health for much of your life, then the process may be a little more challenging, but there are still many things that you can do to help ease the transition.

Because this transition is so unique for each woman, you will again derive more benefit from a program that is tailored for you by an experienced Ayurvedic practitioner. There are also a number of books that will give you direction, including Atreya's book *Ayurvedic Healing for Women*. Below are a few general tips to keep in mind as you pass through this phase of life.

Tips for Menopause

Diet and herbs. Because Vata is high during menopause, you'll want to follow a diet that is Vata reducing, particularly if you are already a Vata type. However, if you are also prone to Pitta symptoms of heat, like hot flashes, then you'll want to be careful to not provoke Pitta further with too many warming or spicy foods. Atreya recommends that your diet be low in animal proteins, as these will rob your body of much-needed calcium. He also suggests using the herb triphala, which is good for all three constitutions and helps to maintain the colon. Vasant Lad recommends taking a teaspoon of fresh aloe vera gel three times a day to help prevent and relieve uncomfortable symptoms. In general, herbal formulas can be very helpful during this phase, so you'll want to consult other sources for this information.

Exercise and yoga. Because the body tends to get weaker and less flexible with age, it's important to maintain, or begin, a program of moderate or gentle exercise. Walking is one of the safest forms of exercise and will help keep your joints and muscles limber and strong while at the same time working your lungs. Swimming is another form of exercise that may appeal to you, particularly if you are a Pitta type or if your bones feel fragile and need more support. Your yoga practice should be modified to a more gentle routine. It may also be appropriate for you to emphasize postures that are good for a Vata type; these include postures that help maintain the health of the colon. (See chapter 5 for more details on yoga practice.) Also, if you are not practicing yoga but are interested in learning, you may want to find a teacher. You will derive more benefit from working with a teacher who has experience working with women in menopause; you may also find yourself drawn to studying with a teacher who is close to your age.

Abhyanga and massage. Abhyanga, or self-massage, will help to nourish and replenish the skin, which tends to get so dry in later years. Also, through the physical action of massaging yourself, you'll keep your body somewhat limber. If you can afford to get a massage, this is a good thing to treat yourself to, particularly if you are going through a difficult patch in which uncomfortable symptoms are arising.

Pranayama and meditation. It is never too late to bring wonderful breathing and meditation practices into your life. In fact, at this stage of life, it is recommended that you spend more time turning inward with the practice of meditation. Older people in India traditionally become much more spiritually oriented at this time in their lives; they are not expected to perform their usual household duties, and some even embark on long pilgrimages. See chapter 5 for suggestions on meditation, or, if you already have your own method, follow that. You may also want to work with pranayama practices, either emphasizing cooling or warming breaths, depending on your needs; these are also listed in chapter 5.

Ayurveda views menstruation, pregnancy, and menopause as normal and natural phases of a woman's life, and as such, they need not be fraught with difficulty. Problems can arise when we unwittingly live in ways that go against our nature. Some of the stressors in our lives that contribute to our difficulties are, of course, beyond our control. But many of them are things that we can address and change ourselves. The beauty of Ayurveda is that it gives us simple tools that can be worked into our lives to help us realign ourselves with our own nature. An understanding of these lifestyle choices, combined with a little patience and willingness to change, empowers each of us to become healthier, happier women, even in the midst of challenging circumstances.

ACKNOWLEDGMENTS

Many people have helped birth *Ayurveda Wisdom*. I am grateful to the wonderful staff at Conari, with special thanks going to Leslie Berriman, whose enthusiasm for this book made it possible in the first place. I am very grateful to my editor, Heather McArthur, who was extremely patient, supportive, and helpful. Priscilla Stuckey also provided a number of useful editing suggestions. Thanks to Suzanne Albertson for a beautifully designed cover and to all the others at Conari who have contributed in one way or another to this project.

I owe a great debt to the many teachers and authors whose books, articles, and private consultations have made Ayurveda more accessible to me. Many thanks also go to my father-in-law, Rajendra Bhansali, who provided stimulating conversation about both Ayurveda and yoga.

TO LEARN MORE

Ayurveda is a vast and complex subject, and many other aspects of this ancient tradition are not touched upon in this book. If you want to explore further, the sources listed below will provide you with useful information. These sources include several books on yoga, which is closely related to Ayurveda.

BOOKS AND ARTICLES

Anselmo, Peter, with James S. Brooks, MD. *Ayurvedic Secrets to Longevity and Total Health.* Paramus, NJ: Prentice-Hall, 1996.

Atreya. *Ayurvedic Healing for Women.* York Beach, ME: Samuel Weiser, 1999.

_____. *Practical Ayurveda: Secrets for Physical, Sexual, and Spiritual Health.* York Beach, ME: Samuel Weiser, 1998.

Chopra, Deepak, MD. *Perfect Health: The Complete Mind/Body Guide.* New York: Harmony Books, 1991.

Desikachar, T. K. V. *The Heart of Yoga.* Rochester, VT: Inner Traditions International, 1995.

Douillard, John. *Body, Mind and Sport.* New York: Harmony, 1992.

Feuerstein, Georg. *The Yoga Tradition: Its History, Literature, Philosophy, and Practice.* Prescott, AZ: Hohm Press, 1998.

Feuerstein, Georg.and Stephan Bodian, eds. *Living Yoga: A Comprehensive Guide for Daily Life.* New York: Tarcher, 1993.

Frawley, David, OMD. *Ayurveda and the Mind.* Twin Lakes, WI: Lotus Press, 1996.

_____. *Ayurvedic Healing: A Comprehensive Guide.* Delhi: Private Limited, 1989.

_____. *Yoga and Ayurveda: Self-Healing and Self-Realization.* Twin Lakes, WI: Lotus Press, 1999.

Gerson, Scott, MD. *Ayurveda: the Ancient Indian Healing Art.* Boston: Element Books, 1993.

Green, Anne. *Thorson's Principles of Ayurveda.* London: Thorsons, 2000.

Lad, Vasant. *Ayurveda: The Science of Self-Healing.* Santa Fe, NM: Lotus Press, 1984.

_____. *The Complete Book of Ayurvedic Home Remedies.* New York: Three Rivers Press, 1998.

_____. *Secrets of the Pulse: The Ancient Art of Ayurvedic Pulse Diagnosis.* Albuquerque, NM: Ayurvedic Press, 1996.

Lad, Vasant, and David Frawley. *The Yoga of Herbs: An Ayurvedic Guide to Herbal Medicine.* Santa Fe, NM: Lotus Press, 1986.

Lad, Vasant, and Usha Lad. *Ayurvedic Cooking for Self-Healing.* Albuquerque, NM: Ayurvedic Press, 1994.

Lansdorf, Nancy, MD, Veronica Butler, MD, and Melanie Brown, PhD. *A Woman's Best Medicine: Health, Happiness, and Long*

Life Through Maharishi Ayur-Veda. New York: Tarcher, 1995.

Lark, Susan M., MD. *PMS: Premenstrual Syndrome Self-Help Book*. Berkeley, CA: Celestial Arts, 1984.

Miller, Richard, PhD. *The Psychophysiology of Respiration: Eastern and Western Perspectives*. Sebastopol, CA: Anahata Press.

Morningstar, Amadea, with Urmila Desai. *The Ayurvedic Cookbook*. Wilmot, WI: Lotus Light, 1990.

Northrup, Christiane, MD. *Women's Bodies, Women's Wisdom*. New York: Bantam Books, 1994.

Patnaik, Naveen. *The Garden of Life: An Introduction to the Healing Plants of India*. Hammersmith, London: Aquarian, 1993.

Schiffmann, Erich. *Yoga: The Spirit and Practice of Moving into Stillness*. New York: Pocket Books, 1996.

Shah, J. T. *Therapeutic Yoga*. Mumbai, India: Vakils, Feffer and Simons, 1999.

Shanbhag, Vivek, MD. *A Beginner's Introduction to Ayurvedic Medicine*. New Canaan, CT: Keats Publishing, 1994.

Svoboda, Robert E. *Ayurveda for Women: A Guide to Vitality and Health*. Devon, England: David & Charles, 1999.

____. *The Hidden Secret of Ayurveda*. Albuquerque, NM: Ayurvedic Press, 1996.

Svoboda, Robert E. and Arnie Lane. *Tao and Dharma: Chinese Medicine and Ayurveda*. Twin Lakes, WI: Lotus Press, 1995.

Tiwari, Maya. *Ayurveda: Secrets of Healing*. Twin Lakes, WI: Lotus Press, 1995.

____. *The Path of Practice: A Woman's Book of Healing with Food, Breath, and Sound*. New York: Ballantine, 2000.

Vanhowten, Donald. *Ayurveda and Life Impressions Bodywork*.

Twin Lakes, WI: Lotus Press, 1996.

Warrier, Gopi, and Deepika Gunawant, MD. *The Complete Illustrated Guide to Ayurveda*. Rockport, MA: Element Books, 1997.

OTHER SOURCES

The Ayurvedic Institute
P.O. Box 23445
Albuquerque, NM 87192
(505) 291-9698

Maharishi Ayur-Veda Medical Center (The Raj)
1734 Jasmine Avenue
Fairfield, IA 52556
(641) 471-9580

National Institute of Ayurvedic Medicine (NIAM)
584 Milltown Road
Brewster, NY 10509
(845) 278-8700

New England Institute of Ayurvedic Medicine
111 North Elm Street, Suites 103–105
Worcester, MA 01609
(508) 755-3744

INDEX

chronic fatigue syndrome, 68

clairvoyance, 18

cleansing programs. *See* panchakarma

coarseness, 16–17

coffee, 28, 52

cold, sensitivity to, 17, 19, 20, 21,
29, 120

colds, 5, 27, 30, 43, 47, 71, 96, 140

colon, 13, 94, 154, 155
   basti and, 99

color therapy, 101, 120
   Kaphas and, 121–22
   Pittas and, 121
   Vatas and, 120–21

*Complete Book of Ayurvedic Home
   Remedies, The* (Lad), 74, 122–23,
   130, 147–48

congestion, 96

constipation, 16, 17, 19, 20, 44, 70,
72, 144, 153

constitution(s), 12. *See also* doshas;
   specific doshas
   classification of, 7
   discovering your, 11–13
   original, 12
   varying, 6

cookbooks, Ayurvedic, 44

day,
   suggested routines for, 132–36

depression, 15, 28, 30, 68, 88,
145, 153

Desai, Urmila, 44, 64

detoxification programs. *See* panchakarma

diabetes, 27, 30

diarrhea, 48, 49, 144

diet
   and doshic imbalance, 67, 77
   during menopause, 154
   during menses, 146–47
   during pregnancy, 150–51

dietary guidelines
   for doshas, 51
   Kapha, 60–63
   Pitta, 55–59
   Vata, 52–55

digestion, 17, 22, 24, 26, 27, 29, 47,
48, 88. *See also* ama; agni
   about, 41–42
   agni and, 41
   ama and, 42

dinner
   recommended times for, 137

disease(s), 3, 42, 67, 115. *See also*
illness
   accumulation phase of, 73
   aggravated/disturbed phase of,
      73
   chronic disease phase of, 74
   doshic imbalance and, 41,

ABOUT THE AUTHOR

Cybèle Tomlinson directs the Berkeley Yoga Center, where she teaches a variety of classes and workshops. She is also a bodyworker with a private practice, and she teaches infant massage to new parents. Cybèle is the author of *Simple Yoga* and writes occasionally for *Yoga Journal*. She lives with her family in Berkeley, California.

A Simple Wisdom Book

Ayurveda Wisdom is part of Conari Press' A Simple Wisdom Book series which seeks to provide accessible books on enlightening topics.

Other titles in the Simple Wisdom Book series:

Simple Meditation & Relaxation
by Joel Levey and Michelle Levey

Simple Feng Shui by Damian Sharp

Simple Kabbalah by Kim Zetter

Simple Chinese Astrology by Damian Sharp

Simple Yoga by Cybèle Tomlinson

Simple Wicca by Michele Morgan

Simple Numerology by Damian Sharp

CONARI PRESS
2550 Ninth Street, Suite 101
Berkeley, California 94710-2551
800-685-9595   510-649-7175
fax: 510-649-7190   e-mail: conari@conari.com
www.conari.com